英文版

THE BOOK OF TEA

Tenshin Okakura

岡倉天心＝著

The Book of Tea is a slight volume,
like the diaphanous wings of an insect,
and yet once those delicate wings quiver,
the essence of the Japanese spirit
echoes far and wide.

IBCパブリッシング

装丁　PARK. Sutherland Inc.
茶の湯イラスト　テッド・高橋
写真　AFLO (p.121)

Echoes of an Art of Life

In the five years after he turned forty-one in 1902, Tenshin Okakura published four books one after another: *The Awakening of the East, The Ideals of the East, The Awakening of Japan*, and *The Book of Tea*. All of these were written in English. Among them, *The Book of Tea* is a slight volume, like the diaphanous wings of an insect, and yet once those delicate wings quiver, the essence of the Japanese spirit echoes far and wide.

In the twenty years prior to writing these works, Okakura founded, together with Ernest Fenollosa, the Tokyo Fine Arts School, now Tokyo University of Fine Arts and Music, helped form the Japan Fine Arts Academy, and through many twists and turns, advocated the excellence of Japan and Japanese arts.

Still he remained bitter that what he attempted to call attention to was recognized neither in Japan nor abroad. Therefore, he attempted first to delineate Japan's position within Asia, and then to explain broadly what Japan's role was. This was the purpose of the first three volumes, but shortly following their publication, war broke out between Japan and Russia. The Russo-Japanese War ended in an unprecedented victory for Japan, and that brought forth an entirely new challenge. He became concerned that this might bring unexpected misunderstandings regarding Japan. Thinking that in order to communicate the spirit of Japan it would be better to describe the aesthetic and ordinary perceptiveness alive within the Japanese people, Okakura did an about-face. What emerged from this change was *The Book of Tea*, which was published in New York in 1906.

The organization of the volume is superb. In the opening section, Tenshin is unable to conceal his irritation when he writes, "When will the West understand, or try to understand, the East?" He then goes on to contrast the West's exclusive emphasis on material and reason with an explanation of how Japan esteems aesthetic appreciation and introspection. From this perspective, he welcomes and entices the reader into the world of tea.

Following this, he sets forth the spirit of tea by touching on several aspects. What makes *The*

Book of Tea different from so many current-day introductions to tea-ceremony is that he offers a carefully outlined argument that tea constitutes the base of a sense of values that was founded in Chinese Taoism and Zen and was created independently in Japan. Upon this major premise, he then argues that the Japanese have, through tea, come to value above all else "Symbolism and Relativity."

The first time I read *The Book of Tea* was when I was a university student. Having grown up in Kyoto in a household selling kimono fabrics and that had its own tea house, I found Tenshin's explanations entirely beyond me. However, as my views of Japan matured, I increasingly became convinced that Tenshin's explanations manifested the fundamental, vital underpinnings of the Japanese today.

There are three points in his work that I would like to call attention to. First is that tea is "an Art of Life," and therefore it is always in touch with the present. Tenshin writes that in tea, this has no beginning and no end.

He also shows that through tea one can transcend the self. While this may smack of a slightly deliberate ridicule of the West's rational self, it would seem to be rather an essential aspect in

Tenshin's argument for a broadly Eastern "Abode of Vacancy," or the mediacy of emptiness.

Thirdly—and this is the message that echoes so strongly within me—he has astutely observed that it was through tea that the Japanese learned the value of "incompleteness." Regardless of the specific case in question, to learn something "incompletely" means not to equate everything as complete in and of itself but to deal with it with a certain supplementary imagination.

Upon close reading, one will discover that a waka and a haiku are introduced in the text.

> *I looked beyond;*
> *Flowers are not,*
> *Nor tinted leaves.*
> *On the sea beach*
> *A solitary cottage stands*
> *In the waning light*
> *Of an autumn eve.*

> *A cluster of summer trees,*
> *A bit of the sea,*
> *A pale evening moon.*

Sen no Rikiu and Kobori-Enshiu, respectively, claimed that each poem conveyed the spirit of tea. In these poems, the fact that the scene before one is incomplete implies and suggests that unlimited powers of imagination are at work. If anything, this is what Tenshin hoped to say in writing this book.

What Tenshin was setting forth in *The Book of Tea* was not instructions on tea-ceremony or etiquette. Rather, he was propounding an outline of the spiritual make-up cultivated within the Japanese people through the way of tea as "an Art of Living." This book can easily be read straight through in a few hours, and yet it is a volume that even today brings to both Japanese and non-Japanese profound reverberations.

Seigow Matsuoka

Seigow Matsuoka 松岡正剛

Having served as the chief editor of the magazine *Yu*, visiting professor to the University of Tokyo, and professor at Tezukayama University, Seigow Matsuoka is now head of the Editorial Engineering Laboratory and principal of the editorial school ISIS. He has established a system of editorial engineering that can be applied to such information-culture fields as Japanese culture, arts, life philosophy, and system engineering. He is actively engaged in such wide-ranging projects as system development, business planning, the revitalization of local cultures, and other fields.

CONTENTS

Echoes of an Art of Life 3

CHAPTER 1
The Cup of Humanity 11

CHAPTER 2
The Schools of Tea 31

CHAPTER 3
Taoism and Zennism 51

CHAPTER 4
The Tea-Room 75

CHAPTER 5
Art Appreciation 103

CHAPTER 6
Flowers 121

CHAPTER 7
Tea-Masters 147

Tea Ceremony 159

Chapter 1
The Cup of Humanity

The Cup of Humanity

Tea ennobled into Teaism, a religion of æstheticism, the adoration of the beautiful among everyday facts – Teaism developed among both nobles and peasants – The mutual misunderstanding of the New World and the Old – The Worship of Tea in the West – Early records of Tea in European writing – The Taoists' version of the combat between Spirit and Matter – The modern struggle for wealth and power.

*T*ea began as a medicine and grew into a beverage. In China, in the eighth century, it entered the realm of poetry as one of the polite amusements. The fifteenth century saw Japan ennoble it into a religion of æstheticism—Teaism. Teaism is a cult founded on the adoration of the beautiful among the sordid facts of everyday existence. It inculcates purity and harmony, the mystery of mutual charity, the romanticism of the social order. It is essentially a worship of the Imperfect, as it is a tender attempt to accomplish something possible in this impossible thing we know as life.

The Philosophy of Tea is not mere æstheticism in the ordinary acceptance of the term, for it expresses conjointly with ethics and religion our whole point of view about man and nature. It is hygiene, for it enforces cleanliness; it is economics, for it shows comfort in simplicity

☐ ennoble 高尚にする ☐ æstheticism 唯美主義 ☐ Teaism 茶道 ☐ sordid 俗な ☐ inculcates 〜に教え込む ☐ conjointly 共同して ☐ hygiene 衛生学

rather than in the complex and costly; it is moral geometry, inasmuch as it defines our sense of proportion to the universe. It represents the true spirit of Eastern democracy by making all its votaries aristocrats in taste.

The long isolation of Japan from the rest of the world, so conducive to introspection, has been highly favourable to the development of Teaism. Our home and habits, costume and cuisine, porcelain, lacquer, painting—our very literature—all have been subject to its influence. No student of Japanese culture could ever ignore its presence. It has permeated the elegance of noble boudoirs, and entered the abode of the humble. Our peasants have learned to arrange flowers, our meanest labourer to offer his salutation to the rocks and waters. In our common parlance we speak of the man "with no tea" in him, when he is insusceptible to the seriocomic

□ inasmuch as ～だから　□ votary 信奉者　□ aristocrat 貴族階級の人
□ conducive 伝導性の　□ cuisine 料理、食事　□ permeate ～に浸透する
□ boudoir 婦人の私室《仏語》　□ meanest labourer 最下層の労働者
□ salutation 礼　□ parlance 言い回し　□ insusceptible 無神経な
□ seriocomic 真面目だが喜劇的な

interests of the personal drama. Again we stigmatise the untamed æsthete who, regardless of the mundane tragedy, runs riot in the springtide of emancipated emotions, as one "with too much tea" in him.

The outsider may indeed wonder at this seeming much ado about nothing. What a tempest in a tea-cup! he will say. But when we consider how small after all the cup of human enjoyment is, how soon overflowed with tears, how easily drained to the dregs in our quenchless thirst for infinity, we shall not blame ourselves for making so much of the tea-cup. Mankind has done worse. In the worship of Bacchus, we have sacrificed too freely; and we have even transfigured the gory image of Mars. Why not consecrate ourselves to the queen of the Camelias, and revel in the warm stream of sympathy that flows from her altar? In the liquid

□stigmatise 非難する　□untamed 自由な　□æsthete 唯美主義者　□springtide 大潮　□emancipate 束縛から解放する　□ado 面倒　□dreg 少量　□quenchless 抑えられない　□Bacchus バッカス《ギリシア神話の酒の神》　□transfigure 〜を美化する　□gory 血なまぐさい　□Mars マルス《ローマ神話の戦いの神》　□Camelia 椿《ツバキ科に属する茶を暗示している》　□revel 大いに楽しむ

amber within the ivory-porcelain, the initiated may touch the sweet reticence of Confucius, the piquancy of Laotse, and the ethereal aroma of Sakyamuni himself.

Those who cannot feel the littleness of great things in themselves are apt to overlook the greatness of little things in others. The average Westerner, in his sleek complacency, will see in the tea-ceremony but another instance of the thousand and one oddities which constitute the quaintness and childishness of the East to him. He was wont to regard Japan as barbarous while she indulged in the gentle arts of peace: he calls her civilised since she began to commit wholesale slaughter on Manchurian battlefields. Much comment has been given lately to the Code of the Samurai,—the Art of Death which makes our soldiers exult in self-sacrifice; but scarcely any attention has been drawn to Teaism, which

☐ amber 琥珀色　☐ reticence 寡黙　☐ Confucius 孔子　☐ piquancy 小粋さ　☐ Laotse 老子　☐ Sakyamuni 釈迦　☐ apt 〜しがちで　☐ complacency 独りよがり　☐ oddity 奇妙なもの［人］　☐ quaintness 古風で趣があること　☐ wont 〜するのを常としている　☐ barbarous 野蛮な　☐ Manchurian 満州　☐ Code of the Samurai 武士道　☐ exult 意気揚々とする

represents so much of our Art of Life. Fain would we remain barbarians, if our claim to civilisation were to be based on the gruesome glory of war. Fain would we await the time when due respect shall be paid to our art and ideals.

When will the West understand, or try to understand, the East? We Asiatics are often appalled by the curious web of facts and fancies which has been woven concerning us. We are pictured as living on the perfume of the lotus, if not on mice and cockroaches. It is either impotent fanaticism or else abject voluptuousness. Indian spirituality has been derided as ignorance, Chinese sobriety as stupidity, Japanese patriotism as the result of fatalism. It has been said that we are less sensible to pain and wounds on account of the callousness of our nervous organisation!

Why not amuse yourselves at our expense?

☐ fain 喜んで　☐ Asiatic アジア人　☐ appall 〜をぎょっとさせる　☐ lotus 蓮
☐ cockroache ゴキブリ　☐ fanaticism 狂信　☐ abject いやしむべき
☐ voluptuousness 心地よさ、官能的なこと　☐ deride 〜をあざける
☐ sobriety 真面目だが喜劇的な　☐ callousness 無感覚

Asia returns the compliment. There would be further food for merriment if you were to know all that we have imagined and written about you. All the glamour of the perspective is there, all the unconscious homage of wonder, all the silent resentment of the new and undefined. You have been loaded with virtues too refined to be envied, and accused of crimes too picturesque to be condemned. Our writers in the past—the wise men who knew—informed us that you had bushy tails somewhere hidden in your garments, and often dined off a fricassee of newborn babes! Nay, we had something worse against you: we used to think you the most impracticable people on the earth, for you were said to preach what you never practised.

Such misconceptions are fast vanishing amongst us. Commerce has forced the European tongues on many an Eastern port. Asiatic youths

□ compliment 賛辞　□ merriment 面白がって笑うこと　□ glamour 魅力
□ homage 敬意　□ resentment 恨み　□ picturesque 人目を引く　□ condemn 非難する　□ dine off 〜を夕食に食べる　□ fricassee 細切れ肉のシチュー
□ impracticable 実行に移すことのできない

are flocking to Western colleges for the equipment of modern education. Our insight does not penetrate your culture deeply, but at least we are willing to learn. Some of my compatriots have adopted too much of your customs and too much of your etiquette, in the delusion that the acquisition of stiff collars and tall silk hats comprised the attainment of your civilisation. Pathetic and deplorable as such affectations are, they evince our willingness to approach the West on our knees. Unfortunately the Western attitude is unfavourable to the understanding of the East. The Christian missionary goes to impart, but not to receive. Your information is based on the meagre translations of our immense literature, if not on the unreliable anecdotes of passing travellers. It is rarely that the chivalrous pen of a Lafcadio Hearn or that of the author of *The Web of Indian Life* enlivens the Oriental

---

□compatriot 同国人　□delusion 思い違い　□attainment 到達　□pathetic 哀れを誘う　□deplorable 嘆かわしい　□affectation 虚飾　□impart ～を分け与える　□anecdote 逸話　□chivalrous 騎士道的な　□Lafcadio Hearn ラフカディオ・ハーン《1850–1904、作家。小泉八雲の本名》　□The Web of Indian Life『インド生活の仕組み』《ニヴェディタ著》

darkness with the torch of our own sentiments.

Perhaps I betray my own ignorance of the Tea Cult by being so outspoken. Its very spirit of politeness exacts that you say what you are expected to say, and no more. But I am not to be a polite Teaist. So much harm has been done already by the mutual misunderstanding of the New World and the Old, that one need not apologise for contributing his tithe to the furtherance of a better understanding. The beginning of the twentieth century would have been spared the spectacle of sanguinary warfare if Russia had condescended to know Japan better. What dire consequences to humanity lie in the contemptuous ignoring of Eastern problems! European imperialism, which does not disdain to raise the absurd cry of the Yellow Peril, fails to realise that Asia may also awaken to the cruel sense of the White Disaster. You may laugh at us

---

☐ betray 〜をうっかり表す　☐ tithe 十分の一税《わずかのものの比喩》
☐ furtherance 促進　☐ sanguinary 血なまぐさい　☐ condescend 謙虚な行動をとる　☐ dire 恐ろしい　☐ contemptuous 軽蔑的な　☐ imperialism 帝国主義　☐ disdain 〜を恥とする　☐ Yellow Peril 黄禍《黄色人種が白色人種を脅かすという禍害》　☐ White Disaster 白禍《白色人種が黄色人種を脅かすという禍害》

for having "too much tea," but may we not suspect that you of the West have "no tea" in your constitution?

Let us stop the continents from hurling epigrams at each other, and be sadder if not wiser by the mutual gain of half a hemisphere. We have developed along different lines, but there is no reason why one should not supplement the other. You have gained expansion at the cost of restlessness; we have created a harmony which is weak against aggression. Will you believe it?—the East is better off in some respects than the West!

Strangely enough humanity has so far met in the tea-cup. It is the only Asiatic ceremonial which commands universal esteem. The white man has scoffed at our religion and our morals, but has accepted the brown beverage without hesitation. The afternoon tea is now an

□ epigram 警句 □ hemisphere（地球の）半球 □ restlessness 不穏状態
□ aggression 侵略 □ esteem 尊敬（されていること） □ scoff あざ笑う

important function in Western society. In the delicate clatter of trays and saucers, in the soft rustle of feminine hospitality, in the common catechism about cream and sugar, we know that the Worship of Tea is established beyond question. The philosophic resignation of the guest to the fate awaiting him in the dubious decoction proclaims that in this single instance the Oriental spirit reigns supreme.

The earliest record of tea in European writing is said to be found in the statement of an Arabian traveller, that after the year 879 the main sources of revenue in Canton were the duties on salt and tea. Marco Polo records the deposition of a Chinese minister of finance in 1285 for his arbitrary augmentation of the tea-taxes. It was at the period of the great discoveries that the European people began to know more about the extreme Orient. At the end of the sixteenth century the

---

□ catechism 問答　□ dubious ～を疑問に思って　□ decoction 煎茶　□ reign supreme 君臨する　□ Canton 広東《中国の地名》　□ Marco Polo マルコ・ポーロ《1254-1324、イタリアの旅行家》　□ deposition 罷免　□ arbitrary 勝手な　□ augmentation 増加

Hollanders brought the news that a pleasant drink was made in the East from the leaves of a bush. The travellers Giovanni Batista Ramusio (1559), L. Almeida (1576), Maffeno (1588), Tareira (1610), also mentioned tea. In the last-named year ships of the Dutch East India Company brought the first tea into Europe. It was known in France in 1636, and reached Russia in 1638. England welcomed it in 1650 and spoke of it as "That excellent and by all physicians approved China drink, called by the Chineans Tcha, and by other nations Tay, alias Tee."

Like all the good things of the world, the propaganda of Tea met with opposition. Heretics like Henry Saville (1678) denounced drinking it as a filthy custom. Jonas Hanway (*Essay on Tea*, 1756) said that men seemed to lose their stature and comeliness, women their beauty through the use of tea. Its cost at the start (about

---

☐ Hollander オランダ人　☐ Giovanni Batista Ramusio ジョバンニ・バチスタ・ラムシオ《イタリアの地理学者》　☐ L. Almeida L. アルメイダ《1525–1583、ポルトガル人の医師、商人》　☐ Maffeno マフェノ　☐ Tareira タレイラ　☐ Dutch East India Company オランダ東インド会社《1602-1799》　☐ physician 医師　☐ alias 別名　☐ heretic 異端者　☐ Henry Saville ヘンリー・サヴィル《イギリスの政治家》　☐ denounce 公然と非難する　☐ filthy 不潔な　☐ Jonas Hanway ジョナス・ハンウェイ《イギリスの慈善活動家》　☐ stature 身長　☐ comeliness 容姿のよさ

fifteen or sixteen shillings a pound) forbade popular consumption, and made it "regalia for high treatments and entertainments, presents being made thereof to princes and grandees." Yet in spite of such drawbacks tea-drinking spread with marvellous rapidity. The coffeehouses of London in the early half of the eighteenth century became, in fact, tea-houses, the resort of wits like Addison and Steele, who beguiled themselves over their "dish of tea." The beverage soon became a necessary of life—a taxable matter. We are reminded in this connection what an important part it plays in modern history. Colonial America resigned herself to oppression until human endurance gave way before the heavy duties laid on Tea. American independence dates from the throwing of tea-chests into Boston harbour.

There is a subtle charm in the taste of tea

□forbade FORBID（〜を許さない）の過去　□regalia 王族の特権　□thereof またはそれに関する　□grandee 高官　□marvellous おどろくべき　□resort of wits 才人のたまり場　□Addison アディソン《1672–1719、イギリスの随筆家、評論家。スティールと新聞スペクテーターを創刊した》　□Steele スティール《1672–1729、イギリスのジャーナリスト》　□beguile 楽しく過ごす　□resign oneself to 〜に甘んじる　□lay on 〜に課税する　□tea-chest 紅茶箱

which makes it irresistible and capable of idealisation. Western humourists were not slow to mingle the fragrance of their thought with its aroma. It has not the arrogance of wine, the self-consciousness of coffee, nor the simpering innocence of cocoa. Already in 1711, says the *Spectator*: "I would therefore in a particular manner recommend these my speculations to all well-regulated families that set apart an hour every morning for tea, bread and butter; and would earnestly advise them for their good to order this paper to be punctually served up and to be looked upon as a part of the tea-equipage." Samuel Johnson draws his own portrait as "a hardened and shameless tea-drinker, who for twenty years diluted his meals with only the infusion of the fascinating plant; who with tea amused the evening, with tea solaced the midnight, and with tea welcomed the morning."

□ humourists ユーモアのある人　□ mingle 〜を混ぜる　□ simper ニタニタ笑う　□ Spectator スペクテーター《1711年3月から12年12月に発行された評論・随筆新聞》　□ speculation 推論　□ well-regulated 規則正しい　□ set apart 取っておく　□ tea-equipage 一式のティーセット　□ Samuel Johnson サミュエル・ジョンソン《1709–1784、イギリスの文学者》　□ dilute (水などで)薄める　□ infusion 浸出液　□ solace 〜を慰める

Charles Lamb, a professed devotee, sounded the true note of Teaism when he wrote that the greatest pleasure he knew was to do a good action by stealth, and to have it found out by accident. For Teaism is the art of concealing beauty that you may discover it, of suggesting what you dare not reveal. It is the noble secret of laughing at yourself, calmly yet thoroughly, and is thus humour itself,—the smile of philosophy. All genuine humourists may in this sense be called tea philosophers,—Thackeray, for instance, and, of course, Shakespeare. The poets of the Decadence (when was not the world in decadence?), in their protests against materialism, have, to a certain extent, also opened the way to Teaism. Perhaps nowadays it is in our demure contemplation of the Imperfect that the West and the East can meet in mutual consolation.

The Taoists relate that at the great beginning

□ Charles Lamb チャールズ・ラム《1775-1834、イギリスの作家》　□ professed 公然の　□ devotee 愛好者　□ stealth ひそかな行為　□ conceal 隠す　□ tea philosopher 茶人　□ Thackeray サッカレー《1811-1863、イギリスの作家》　□ Decadence デカダン（派）、退廃派　□ materialism 物質主義　□ demure 控えめな　□ contemplation 熟視　□ mutual consolation 慰め合い

of the No-Beginning, Spirit and Matter met in mortal combat. At last the Yellow Emperor, the Sun of Heaven, triumphed over Shuhyung, the demon of darkness and earth. The Titan, in his death agony, struck his head against the solar vault and shivered the blue dome of jade into fragments. The stars lost their nests, the moon wandered aimlessly among the wild chasms of the night. In despair the Yellow Emperor sought far and wide for the repairer of the Heavens. He had not to search in vain. Out of the Eastern sea rose a queen, the divine Niuka, horn-crowned and dragon-tailed, resplendent in her armour of fire. She welded the five-coloured rainbow in her magic cauldron and rebuilt the Chinese sky. But it is also told that Niuka forgot to fill two tiny crevices in the blue firmament. Thus began the dualism of love—two souls rolling through space and never at rest until they join together

- Yellow Emperor 黄帝《紀元前2510-2448、中国神話伝説上の帝》　- Sun of Heaven 天子《中国・日本で用いられた君主の称号》　- triumph 勝利する　- Shuhyung 祝融《中国神話の火の神》　- Titan タイタン、巨人　- agony 激しい苦痛　- solar vault 太陽光を取り入れるアーチ状の天井　- jade 翡翠《宝石》　- cgasn 深い淵　- in vain 無駄に　- divine 神　- Niuka 女媧《中国神話の人間を作った創造神》　- cauldron 大釜　- crevice 裂け目　- firmament 天空　- dualism 二元論

to complete the universe. Everyone has to build anew his sky of hope and peace.

The heaven of modern humanity is indeed shattered in the Cyclopean struggle for wealth and power. The world is groping in the shadow of egotism and vulgarity. Knowledge is bought through a bad conscience, benevolence practised for the sake of utility. The East and West, like two dragons tossed in a sea of ferment, in vain strive to regain the jewel of life. We need a Niuka again to repair the grand devastation; we await the great Avatar. Meanwhile, let us have a sip of tea. The afternoon glow is brightening the bamboos, the fountains are bubbling with delight, the soughing of the pines is heard in our kettle. Let us dream of evanescence, and linger in the beautiful foolishness of things.

☐ anew あらためて ☐ Cyclopean 一つ目の巨人キュクロプスのような ☐ grope 暗中模索する ☐ egotism 利己主義 ☐ vulgarity 俗悪野卑 ☐ benevolence 仁愛 ☐ ferment 動乱 ☐ devastation 荒廃 ☐ Avatar アヴァターラ《ヒンドゥー教の救済の神》 ☐ bubble 沸騰する ☐ sough ザワザワと音を立てる ☐ pine 松 ☐ evanescence はかなさ ☐ linger 長居する

Chapter 2
The Schools of Tea

The Schools of Tea

The three stages of the evolution of Tea — The Boiled Tea, the Whipped Tea, and the Steeped Tea, representative of the Tang, the Sung, and the Ming dynasties of China — Luwuh, the first apostle of Tea — The Tea-ideals of the three dynasties — To the latter-day Chinese Tea is a delicious beverage, but not an ideal — In Japan Tea is a religion of the art of life.

Tea is a work of art and needs a master hand to bring out its noblest qualities. We have good and bad tea, as we have good and bad paintings—generally the latter. There is no single recipe for making the perfect tea, as there are no rules for producing a Titian or a Sesson. Each preparation of the leaves has its individuality, its special affinity with water and heat, its hereditary memories to recall, its own method of telling a story. The truly beautiful must be always in it. How much do we not suffer through the constant failure of society to recognise this simple and fundamental law of art and life; Lichihlai, a Sung poet, has sadly remarked that there were three most deplorable things in the world: the spoiling of fine youths through false education, the degradation of fine paintings through vulgar admiration, and the utter waste of fine tea through incompetent manipulation.

☐ Titian ティツィアーノ《1490–1576、ルネサンス期イタリアの画家》
☐ Sesson 雪村《1504–1589、室町後期の水墨画家》　☐ affinity 相性
☐ hereditary 先祖代々の　☐ Lichihlai 李竹嬾《中国宋時代の詩人》　☐ Sung 宋《中国王朝のひとつ、960–1279》　☐ degradation 体面を傷つけること　☐ vulgar 品のない　☐ utter まったくの　☐ incompetent 無能な　☐ manipulation 取り扱い

CHAPTER 2 THE SCHOOLS OF TEA

Like Art, Tea has its periods and its schools. Its evolution may be roughly divided into three main stages: the Boiled Tea, the Whipped Tea, and the Steeped Tea. We moderns belong to the last school. These several methods of appreciating the beverage are indicative of the spirit of the age in which they prevailed. For life is an expression, our unconscious actions the constant betrayal of our innermost thought. Confucius said that "man hideth not." Perhaps we reveal ourselves too much in small things because we have so little of the great to conceal. The tiny incidents of daily routine are as much a commentary of racial ideals as the highest flight of philosophy or poetry. Even as the difference in favourite vintage marks the separate idiosyncrasies of different periods and nationalities of Europe, so the Tea-ideals characterise the various moods of Oriental culture. The Cake-tea

---

☐ school 流派 ☐ Boiled Tea 団茶 ☐ Whipped Tea 抹茶 ☐ Steeped Tea 煎茶 ☐ indicative 〜を示して ☐ prevail 流行する ☐ betrayal 裏切り ☐ man hideth not 人いずくんぞかくさんや（人は隠しおおすことができない） ☐ commentary 解説 ☐ racial ideal 民族の理想 ☐ idiosyncrasy 特異性 ☐ Tea-ideal 理想の茶 ☐ Cake-tea 団茶

which was boiled, the Powdered-tea which was whipped, the Leaf-tea which was steeped, mark the distinct emotional impulses of the Tang, the Sung, and the Ming dynasties of China. If we were inclined to borrow the much-abused terminology of art classification, we might designate them respectively, the Classic, the Romantic, and the Naturalistic schools of Tea.

The tea plant, a native of southern China, was known from very early times to Chinese botany and medicine. It is alluded to in the classics under the various names of Tou, Tseh, Chung, Kha, and Ming, and was highly prized for possessing the virtues of relieving fatigue, delighting the soul, strengthening the will, and repairing the eyesight. It was not only administered as an internal dose, but often applied externally in form of paste to alleviate rheumatic pains. The Taoists claimed it as an important ingredient of

---

□Powdered-tea 抹茶　□Leaf-tea 煎茶　□steep ～を浸す　□Tang 唐《中国王朝のひとつ、618-907》　□Ming 明《中国王朝のひとつ、1368-1644》
□terminology 専門用語　□designate ～と名付ける　□botany 植物学
□allude それとなく言及する　□Tou, Tseh, Chung, Kha, and Ming「荼」、「蔎」、「荈」、「檟」、「茗」《いずれも茶の木の別称》　□fatigue 疲労　□internal dose 内服（薬）　□alleviate ～をやわらげる　□rheumatic リウマチの
□Taoist 道教信者

the elixir of immortality. The Buddhists used it extensively to prevent drowsiness during their long hours of meditation.

By the fourth and fifth centuries Tea became a favourite beverage among the inhabitants of the Yangtse-Kiang valley. It was about this time that the modern ideograph Cha was coined, evidently a corruption of the classic Tou. The poets of the southern dynasties have left some fragments of their fervent adoration of the "froth of the liquid jade." Then emperors used to bestow some rare preparation of the leaves on their high ministers as a reward for eminent services. Yet the method of drinking tea at this stage was primitive in the extreme. The leaves were steamed, crushed in a mortar, made into a cake, and boiled together with rice, ginger, salt, orange peel, spices, milk, and sometimes with onions! The custom obtains at the present day among

☐ elixir of immortality 不老不死の薬　☐ drowsiness 眠気　☐ meditation 瞑想　☐ inhabitant 住民　☐ Yangtse-Kiang valley 揚子江流域　☐ ideograph 表意文字　☐ Cha 茶　☐ coin (新しい言葉を)作る　☐ dynasty 王朝　☐ fervent 熱烈な　☐ adoration 賛美　☐ froth 泡　☐ bestow 〜を授ける　☐ high minister 高官　☐ eminent 優れた　☐ primitive 原始的な　☐ mortar すり鉢

the Thibetans and various Mongolian tribes, who make a curious syrup of these ingredients. The use of lemon slices by the Russians, who learned to take tea from the Chinese caravansaries, points to the survival of the ancient method.

It needed the genius of the Tang dynasty to emancipate Tea from its crude state and lead to its final idealisation. With Luwuh in the middle of the eighth century we have our first apostle of tea. He was born in an age when Buddhism, Taoism, and Confucianism were seeking mutual synthesis. The pantheistic symbolism of the time was urging one to mirror the Universal in the Particular. Luwuh, a poet, saw in the Tea-service the same harmony and order which reigned through all things. In his celebrated work, the "Chaking" (*The Holy Scripture of Tea*) he formulated the Code of Tea. He has since been worshipped as the tutelary god of the Chinese tea merchants.

□ Thibetan チベット人の　□ caravansary 隊商宿　□ crude 荒削りな
□ Luwuh 陸羽《733-804、中国唐時代の文筆家》　□ apostle 伝道者　□ Taoism 道教　□ Confucianism 儒教　□ synthesis 統合　□ pantheistic symbolism 汎神論的象徴主義　□ reign 支配する　□ Chaking 茶経《茶の聖典の意》
□ tutelary 守護神

The "Chaking" consists of three volumes and ten chapters. In the first chapter Luwuh treats of the nature of the tea plant, in the second of the implements for gathering the leaves, in the third of the selection of the leaves. According to him the best quality of the leaves must have "creases like the leathern boot of Tartar horsemen, curl like the dew-lap of a mighty bullock, unfold like a mist rising out of a ravine, gleam like a lake touched by a zephyr, and be wet and soft like fine earth newly swept by rain."

The fourth chapter is devoted to the enumeration and description of the twenty-four members of the tea-equipage, beginning with the tripod brazier and ending with the bamboo cabinet for containing all these utensils. Here we notice Luwuh's predilection for Taoist symbolism. Also it is interesting to observe in this connection the influence of tea on Chinese

---

☐ implement 道具　☐ leathern 革製の　☐ Tartar タタール人《中央アジアのモンゴル系民族》　☐ dew-lap のど袋　☐ bullock 若い雄牛　☐ ravine 峡谷　☐ gleam 輝く　☐ zephyr そよ風　☐ tripod brazier 風炉《湯を沸かす炉》

ceramics. The Celestial porcelain, as is well known, had its origin in an attempt to reproduce the exquisite shade of jade, resulting, in the Tang dynasty, in the blue glaze of the south, and the white glaze of the north. Luwuh considered the blue as the ideal colour for the tea-cup, as it lent additional greenness to the beverage, whereas the white made it look pinkish and distasteful. It was because he used cake-tea. Later on, when the tea-masters of Sung took to the powdered tea, they preferred heavy bowls of blue-black and dark brown. The Mings, with their steeped tea, rejoiced in light ware of white porcelain.

In the fifth chapter Luwuh describes the method of making tea. He eliminates all ingredients except salt. He dwells also on the much-discussed question of the choice of water and the degree of boiling it. According to him,

□celestial 最高の　□porcelain 磁器　□glaze 光沢　□eliminate 〜を取り除く　□dwell on 〜について深く論じる

the mountain spring is the best, the river water and the spring water come next in the order of excellence. There are three stages of boiling: the first boil is when the little bubbles like the eye of fishes swim on the surface; the second boil is when the bubbles are like crystal beads rolling in a fountain; the third boil is when the billows surge wildly in the kettle. The Cake-tea is roasted before the fire until it becomes soft like a baby's arm and is shredded into powder between pieces of fine paper. Salt is put in the first boil, the tea in the second. At the third boil, a dipperful of cold water is poured into the kettle to settle the tea and revive the "youth of the water." Then the beverage was poured into cups and drunk. O nectar! The filmy leaflet hung like scaly clouds in a serene sky or floated like water lilies on emerald streams. It was of such a beverage that Lotung, a Tang poet, wrote: "The

□ billow うねり　□ surge 湧き上がる　□ shred 〜を細かくする　□ dipperful ひしゃく一杯　□ O nectar! 甘美な飲み物！《O は OH と同》　□ filmy 薄膜状の　□ scaly うろこ状の　□ serene 晴れた　□ Lotung 盧同《？-835、中国唐時代の詩人》

first cup moistens my lips and throat, the second cup breaks my loneliness, the third cup searches my barren entrail but to find therein some five thousand volumes of odd ideographs. The fourth cup raises a slight perspiration,—all the wrong of life passes away through my pores. At the fifth cup I am purified; the sixth cup calls me to the realms of immortals. The seventh cup—ah, but I could take no more! I only feel the breath of cool wind that rises in my sleeves. Where is Horaisan? Let me ride on this sweet breeze and waft away thither."

The remaining chapters of the "Chaking" treat of the vulgarity of the ordinary methods of tea-drinking, a historical summary of illustrious tea-drinkers, the famous tea plantations of China, the possible variations of the tea-service, and illustrations of the tea-utensils. The last is unfortunately lost.

☐ barren 荒野 ☐ perspiration 発汗 ☐ pore 毛穴 ☐ Horaisan 蓬莱山《中国にある仙人が住むという山》 ☐ waft フワフワと飛ぶ ☐ thither そこへ ☐ illustrious 高名な ☐ tea-utensil 茶道具

The appearance of the "Chaking" must have created considerable sensation at the time. Luwuh was befriended by the Emperor Taisung (763–779), and his fame attracted many followers. Some exquisites were said to have been able to detect the tea made by Luwuh from that of his disciples. One mandarin has his name immortalised by his failure to appreciate the tea of this great master.

In the Sung dynasty the whipped tea came into fashion and created the second school of Tea. The leaves were ground to fine powder in a small stone mill, and the preparation was whipped in hot water by a delicate whisk made of split bamboo. The new process led to some change in the teaequipage of Luwuh, as well as the choice of leaves. Salt was discarded forever. The enthusiasm of the Sung people for tea knew no bounds. Epicures vied with each other in

□ Emperor Taisung 代宗帝《763–779、中国唐時代の皇帝》 □ disciple 弟子 □ mandarin 上級官吏 □ immortalise 〜の名を不滅にする □ came into fashion 流行する □ whisk 泡立て器 □ discard 解雇する □ epicure 美食家 □ vie 競う

discovering new varieties, and regular tournaments were held to decide their superiority. The Emperor Kiasung (1101–1124), who was too great an artist to be a well-behaved monarch, lavished his treasures on the attainment of rare species. He himself wrote a dissertation on the twenty kinds of tea, among which he prizes the "white tea" as of the rarest and finest quality.

The tea-ideal of the Sungs differed from the Tangs even as their notion of life differed. They sought to actualise what their predecessors tried to symbolise. To the Neo-Confucian mind the cosmic law was not reflected in the phenomenal world, but the phenomenal world was the cosmic law itself. Æons were but moments—Nirvana always within grasp. The Taoist conception that immortality lay in the eternal change permeated all their modes of thought. It was the process, not the deed, which was

☐ Emperor Kiasung 徽宗帝《1101-1124、中国北宋の皇帝》 ☐ monarch 皇帝
☐ lavish 〜を気前よく使う ☐ dissertation 論文 ☐ actualise 実現させる
☐ Neo-Confucian 新儒教 ☐ cosmic law 宇宙の法則 ☐ phenomenal world 現象界《人が知覚できる世界》 ☐ Æons 永劫 ☐ Nirvana 涅槃《悟りを開いた状態》

interesting. It was the completing, not the completion, which was really vital. Man came thus at once face to face with nature. A new meaning grew into the art of life. The tea began to be not a poetical pastime, but one of the methods of self-realisation. Wangyu-cheng eulogised tea as "flooding his soul like a direct appeal, that its delicate bitterness reminded him of the aftertaste of a good counsel." Sotumpa wrote of the strength of the immaculate purity in tea which defied corruption as a truly virtuous man. Among the Buddhists, the southern Zen sect, which incorporated so much of Taoist doctrines, formulated an elaborate ritual of tea. The monks gathered before the image of Bodhi Dharma and drank tea out of a single bowl with the profound formality of a holy sacrament. It was this Zen ritual which finally developed into the Tea-ceremony of Japan in the fifteenth century.

□ pastime 気晴らし　□ Wangyu-cheng 王禹偁《954–1001、中国宋時代の官吏、文人》　□ eulogise 〜を賛美する　□ Sotumpa 蘇東坡《1036–1101、中国北宋の詩人、書家》　□ immaculate 清浄な　□ virtuous 高潔な　□ Zen sect 禅宗　□ doctrine 教義　□ ritual 儀式　□ Bodhi Dharma 菩提達磨《禅宗の開祖とされるインド人仏教僧》　□ sacrament 聖餐　□ Tea-ceremony 茶道

Unfortunately the sudden outburst of the Mongol tribes in the thirteenth century, which resulted in the devastation and conquest of China under the barbaric rule of the Yuen Emperors, destroyed all the fruits of Sung culture. The native dynasty of the Mings which attempted re-nationalisation in the middle of the fifteenth century was harassed by internal troubles, and China again fell under the alien rule of the Manchus in the seventeenth century. Manners and customs changed to leave no vestige of the former times. The powdered tea is entirely forgotten. We find a Ming commentator at loss to recall the shape of the tea whisk mentioned in one of the Sung classics. Tea is now taken by steeping the leaves in hot water in a bowl or cup. The reason why the Western world is innocent of the older method of drinking tea is explained by the fact that Europe

☐ Yuen Emperor 元王朝皇帝　☐ harass 苦しめる　☐ alien 異邦人　☐ Manchu 満州人　☐ vestige 痕跡　☐ at (a) loss 途方にくれて

knew it only at the close of the Ming dynasty.

To the latter-day Chinese tea is a delicious beverage, but not an ideal. The long woes of his country have robbed him of the zest for the meaning of life. He has become modern, that is to say, old and disenchanted. He has lost that sublime faith in illusions which constitutes the eternal youth and vigour of the poets and ancients. He is an eclectic and politely accepts the traditions of the universe. He toys with Nature, but does not condescend to conquer or worship her. His Leaf-tea is often wonderful with its flower-like aroma, but the romance of the Tang and Sung ceremonials are not to be found in his cup.

Japan, which followed closely on the footsteps of Chinese civilisation, has known the tea in all its three stages. As early as the year 729 we read of the Emperor Shomu giving tea to one

☐ woe 災難　☐ zest 強い興味　☐ disenchanted 幻滅した　☐ sublime 崇高な
☐ vigour 活力　☐ eclectic 折衷主義の　☐ Emperor Shomu 聖武天皇《701–756、第45代天皇》

hundred monks at his palace in Nara. The leaves were probably imported by our ambassadors to the Tang Court and prepared in the way then in fashion. In 801 the monk Saicho brought back some seeds and planted them in Yeisan. Many tea-gardens are heard of in the succeeding centuries, as well as the delight of the aristocracy and priesthood in the beverage. The Sung tea reached us in 1191 with the return of Yeisai-zenji, who went there to study the southern Zen school. The new seeds which he carried home were successfully planted in three places, one of which, the Uji district near Kioto, bears still the name of producing the best tea in the world. The southern Zen spread with marvellous rapidity, and with it the tea-ritual and the tea-ideal of the Sung. By the fifteenth Yoshimasa, the tea-ceremony is fully constituted and made into an independent and secular performance. Since

---

☐ Saicho 最澄《767-822、天台宗の開祖》 ☐ Yeisan 比叡山 ☐ succeeding 続く ☐ priesthood 僧職者 ☐ Yeisai-zenji 栄西禅師《1141-1215、臨済宗の開祖》 ☐ Kioto 京都 ☐ tea-ritual 茶の儀式 ☐ tea-ideal 茶の理想 ☐ Yoshimasa（足利）義政《1436-1490、室町幕府第8代将軍》

then Teaism is fully established in Japan. The use of the steeped tea of the later China is comparatively recent among us, being only known since the middle of the seventeenth century. It has replaced the Powdered-tea in ordinary consumption, though the latter still continues to hold its place as the tea of teas.

It is in the Japanese tea-ceremony that we see the culmination of tea-ideals. Our successful resistance of the Mongol invasion in 1281 had enabled us to carry on the Sung movement so disastrously cut off in China itself through the nomadic inroad. Tea with us became more than an idealisation of the form of drinking; it is a religion of the art of life. The beverage grew to be an excuse for the worship of purity and refinement, a sacred function at which the host and guest joined to produce for that occasion the utmost beatitude of the mundane. The tea-room

□ culmination 絶頂　□ Mongol invasion in 1281 元寇（弘安の役）
□ nomadic 遊牧民族の　□ inroad 侵略　□ refinement 洗練　□ beatitude 無上の幸せ　□ mundane この世

was an oasis in the dreary waste of existence where weary travellers could meet to drink from the common spring of art-appreciation. The ceremony was an improvised drama whose plot was woven about the tea, the flowers, and the paintings. Not a colour to disturb the tone of the room, not a sound to mar the rhythm of things, not a gesture to obtrude on the harmony, not a word to break the unity of the surroundings, all movements to be performed simply and naturally—such were the aims of the tea-ceremony. And strangely enough it was often successful. A subtle philosophy lay behind it all. Teaism was Taoism in disguise.

□ dreary 陰鬱な □ improvised 即席の □ mar 台無しにする □ rhythm 韻律 □ obtrude 侵害する □ unity 調和 □ in disguise 姿を変えた

CHAPTER 3
Taoism and Zennism

Taoism and Zennism

The connection of Zennism with Tea – Taoism, and its successor Zennism, represent the individualistic trend of the Southern Chinese mind – Taoism accepts the mundane and tries to find beauty in our world of woe and worry – Zennism emphasizes the teachings of Taoism – Through consecrated meditation may be attained supreme self-realisation – Zennism, like Taoism, is the worship of Relativity – Ideal of Teaism a result of the Zen conception of greatness in the smallest incidents of life – Taoism furnished the basis for æsthetic ideals, Zennism made them practical.

The connection of Zennism with tea is proverbial. We have already remarked that the tea-ceremony was a development of the Zen ritual. The name of Laotse, the founder of Taoism, is also intimately associated with the history of tea. It is written in the Chinese school manual concerning the origin of habits and customs that the ceremony of offering tea to a guest began with Kwanyin, a well-known disciple of Laotse, who first at the gate of the Han Pass presented to the "Old Philosopher" a cup of the golden elixir. We shall not stop to discuss the authenticity of such tales, which are valuable, however, as confirming the early use of the beverage by the Taoists. Our interest in Taoism and Zennism here lies mainly in those ideas regarding life and art which are so embodied in what we call Teaism.

It is to be regretted that as yet there appears

□Zennism 禅　□proverbial よく知られている　□Laotse 老子《前6世紀頃、古代中国の哲学者》　□intimately 密接に　□Kwanyin 関尹《古代中国の伝説的思想家》　□Han Pass 函谷関《中国河南省にある交通の要所》　□authenticity 真偽　□embody 具体化する

to be no adequate presentation of the Taoist and Zen doctrines in any foreign language, though we have had several laudable attempts.

Translation is always a treason, and as a Ming author observes, can at its best be only the reverse side of a brocade,—all the threads are there, but not the subtlety of colour or design. But, after all, what great doctrine is there which is easy to expound? The ancient sages never put their teachings in systematic form. They spoke in paradoxes, for they were afraid of uttering half-truths. They began by talking like fools and ended by making their hearers wise. Laotse himself, with his quaint humour, says, "If people of inferior intelligence hear of the Tao, they laugh immensely. It would not be the Tao unless they laughed at it."

The Tao literally means a Path. It has been severally translated as the Way, the Absolute, the

Law, Nature, Supreme Reason, the Mode. These renderings are not incorrect, for the use of the term by the Taoists differs according to the subject-matter of the inquiry. Laotse himself spoke of it thus: "There is a thing which is all-containing, which was born before the existence of Heaven and Earth. How silent! How solitary! It stands alone and changes not. It revolves without danger to itself and is the mother of the universe. I do not know its name and so call it the Path. With reluctance I call it the Infinite. Infinity is the Fleeting, the Fleeting is the Vanishing, the Vanishing is the Reverting." The Tao is in the Passage rather than the Path. It is the spirit of Cosmic Change,—the eternal growth which returns upon itself to produce new forms. It recoils upon itself like the dragon, the beloved symbol of the Taoists. It folds and unfolds as do the clouds. The Tao might be spoken of as the

☐ rendering 翻訳 ☐ subject-matter 主題 ☐ solitary 孤独の ☐ Fleeting うたかた ☐ Reverting 反転

Great Transition. Subjectively it is the Mood of the Universe. Its Absolute is the Relative.

It should be remembered in the first place that Taoism, like its legitimate successor, Zennism, represents the individualistic trend of the Southern Chinese mind in contradistinction to the communism of Northern China which expressed itself in Confucianism. The Middle Kingdom is as vast as Europe and has a differentiation of idiosyncrasies marked by the two great river systems which traverse it. The Yangtse-Kiang and Hoang-Ho are respectively the Mediterranean and the Baltic. Even today, in spite of centuries of unification, the Southern Celestial differs in his thoughts and beliefs from his Northern brother as a member of the Latin race differs from the Teuton. In ancient days, when communication was even more difficult than at present, and especially during

☐ legitimate　正統の　　☐ contradistinction　対比　　☐ communism　共産主義
☐ The Middle Kingdom　中国　　☐ traverse　～を横切る　　☐ Hoang-Ho　黄河
☐ Mediterranean　地中海　　☐ Baltic　バルト海　　☐ Teuton　チュートン人《古代ゲルマン族の一派》

the feudal period, this difference in thought was most pronounced. The art and poetry of the one breathes an atmosphere entirely distinct from that of the other. In Laotse and his followers and in Kutsugen, the forerunner of the Yangtse-Kiang nature-poets, we find an idealism quite inconsistent with the prosaic ethical notions of their contemporary northern writers. Laotse lived five centuries before the Christian Era.

The germ of Taoist speculation may be found long before the advent of Laotse, surnamed the Long-Eared. The archaic records of China, especially the Book of Changes, foreshadow his thought. But the great respect paid to the laws and customs of that classic period of Chinese civilisation which culminated with the establishment of the Chow dynasty in the twelfth century b.c., kept the development of individualism in check for a long while, so that it was

---

□ feudal period 封建時代　□ pronounce はっきりと表す　□ Kutsugen 屈原《前343-277頃、中国戦国時代の詩人》　□ forerunner 先駆者　□ inconsistent 相容れない　□ prosaic 退屈な　□ ethical 道徳上の　□ advent 出現
□ surnamed 〜というあだ名の　□ Long-Eared 老聃《老子のあだ名》
□ archaic 古代の　□ Book of Changes 易経《儒教の基本五経のひとつ》
□ foreshadow 前兆となる　□ culminate 最高潮に達する　□ Chow dynasty 周王朝《前1046-前256、古代中国の王朝》

not until after the disintegration of the Chow dynasty and the establishment of innumerable independent kingdoms that it was able to blossom forth in the luxuriance of free-thought. Laotse and Soshi (Chuangtse) were both Southerners and the greatest exponents of the New School. On the other hand Confucius with his numerous disciples aimed at retaining ancestral conventions. Taoism cannot be understood without some knowledge of Confucianism and vice versa.

We have said that the Taoist Absolute was the Relative. In ethics the Taoist railed at the laws and the moral codes of society, for to them right and wrong were but relative terms. Definition is always limitation—the "fixed" and "unchangeless" are but terms expressive of a stoppage of growth. Said Kutsugen, "The Sages move the world." Our standards of morality

☐ disintegration 崩壊　☐ innumerable 無数の　☐ luxuriance 豊かさ　☐ Soshi (Chuangtse) 荘子《前369–前286、道教の始祖のひとり》　☐ exponent 主唱者　☐ New School 新思潮《時代を支配する新しい思想傾向》　☐ Taoist Absolute 道教における絶対　☐ rail 非難する　☐ moral codes 道徳規範　☐ unchangeless 不変であること　☐ stoppage 停止

are begotten of the past needs of society, but is society to remain always the same? The observance of communal traditions involves a constant sacrifice of the individual to the state. Education, in order to keep up the mighty delusion, encourages a species of ignorance. People are not taught to be really virtuous, but to behave properly. We are wicked because we are frightfully self-conscious. We never forgive others because we know that we ourselves are in the wrong. We nurse a conscience because we are afraid to tell the truth to others; we take refuge in pride because we are afraid to tell the truth to ourselves. How can one be serious with the world when the world itself is so ridiculous! The spirit of barter is everywhere. Honour and Chastity! Behold the complacent salesman retailing the Good and True. One can even buy a so-called Religion, which is really but common

---

□ begotten BEGET (生み出す) の過去分詞　□ observance 慣習　□ communal 地域社会の　□ wicked 不道徳な　□ frightfully 恐ろしく　□ take refuge in ～に避難する　□ ridiculous ばかげた　□ Chastity 貞節　□ behold ～を見よ　□ complacent 自己満足した

morality sanctified with flowers and music. Rob the Church of her accessories and what remains behind? Yet the trusts thrive marvelously, for the prices are absurdly cheap,—a prayer for a ticket to heaven, a diploma for an honourable citizenship. Hide yourself under a bushel quickly, for if your real usefulness were known to the world you would soon be knocked down to the highest bidder by the public auctioneer. Why do men and women like to advertise themselves so much? Is it not but an instinct derived from the days of slavery?

The virility of the idea lies not less in its power of breaking through contemporary thought than in its capacity for dominating subsequent movements. Taoism was an active power during the Shin dynasty, that epoch of Chinese unification from which we derive the name of China. It would be interesting had we time to note its influence on contemporary thinkers, the mathematicians, writers on law and war, the mystics and alchemists and the later nature-poets of the Yangtse-Kiang. We should not even ignore those speculators on Reality who doubted whether a white horse was real because he was white, or because he was solid, nor the Conversationalists of the Six dynasties who, like the Zen philosophers, revelled in discussions concerning the Pure and the Abstract. Above all we should pay homage to Taoism for what it has done toward the formation of the Celestial character, giving to it a certain capacity for reserve and refinement as "warm as jade." Chinese history is full of instances in which the votaries of Taoism, princes and hermits alike, followed with varied and interesting results the teachings of their creed. The tale will not be without its quota of instruction and amusement. It will be rich in

---

□ mystic 神秘主義者　□ alchemist 錬金術師　□ Conversationalist 清談家
□ the Pure and the Abstract「純粋」と「抽象」　□ hermit 隠遁者　□ creed 教義　□ quota 割り当て

anecdotes, allegories, and aphorisms. We would fain be on speaking terms with the delightful emperor who never died because he never lived. We may ride the wind with Liehtse and find it absolutely quiet because we ourselves are the wind, or dwell in mid-air with the Aged One of the Hoang-Ho, who lived betwixt Heaven and Earth because he was subject to neither the one nor the other. Even in that grotesque apology for Taoism which we find in China at the present day, we can revel in a wealth of imagery impossible to find in any other cult.

But the chief contribution of Taoism to Asiatic life has been in the realm of æsthetics. Chinese historians have always spoken of Taoism as the "art of being in the world," for it deals with the present—ourselves. It is in us that God meets with Nature, and yesterday parts from tomorrow. The Present is the moving Infinity,

□ allegory 寓話　□ aphorism 警句　□ Liehtse 列子《中国春秋戦国時代の道家》
□ Aged One of the Hoang-Ho 黄河の中空に住むと言われている老人
□ betwixt BETWEEN の古語　□ be subject to 〜の支配下にある　□ grotesque 奇怪な　□ apology 名ばかりのもの　□ imagery 比喩　□ æsthetic 美学

the legitimate sphere of the Relative. Relativity seeks Adjustment; Adjustment is Art. The art of life lies in a constant readjustment to our surroundings. Taoism accepts the mundane as it is and, unlike the Confucians and the Buddhists, tries to find beauty in our world of woe and worry. The Sung allegory of the Three Vinegar Tasters explains admirably the trend of the three doctrines. Sakyamuni, Confucius, and Laotse once stood before a jar of vinegar—the emblem of life—and each dipped in his fingers to taste the brew. The matter-of-fact Confucius found it sour, the Buddha called it bitter, and Laotse pronounced it sweet.

The Taoists claimed that the comedy of life could be made more interesting if everyone would preserve the unities. To keep the proportion of things and give place to others without losing one's own position was the secret of

---

□ legitimate sphere　正当な活動領域　□ Three Vinegar Tasters 『酢を味わう3人』《中国宋代の寓話》　□ matter-of-fact　率直な

success in the mundane drama. We must know the whole play in order to properly act our parts; the conception of totality must never be lost in that of the individual. This Laotse illustrates by his favourite metaphor of the Vacuum. He claimed that only in vacuum lay the truly essential. The reality of a room, for instance, was to be found in the vacant space enclosed by the roof and walls, not in the roof and walls themselves. The usefulness of a water pitcher dwelt in the emptiness where water might be put, not in the form of the pitcher or the material of which it was made. Vacuum is all potent because all containing. In vacuum alone motion becomes possible. One who could make of himself a vacuum into which others might freely enter would become master of all situations. The whole can always dominate the part.

These Taoists' ideas have greatly influenced

☐ conception of totality 全体の構想　☐ metaphor 隠喩　☐ Vacuum 虚、真空
☐ dwelt DWELL（宿る）の過去・過去分詞　☐ potent 有力な

all our theories of action, even to those of fencing and wrestling. Jiu-jitsu, the Japanese art of self-defence, owes its name to a passage in the Taoteiking. In jiu-jitsu one seeks to draw out and exhaust the enemy's strength by non-resistance, vacuum, while conserving one's own strength for victory in the final struggle. In art the importance of the same principle is illustrated by the value of suggestion. In leaving something unsaid the beholder is given a chance to complete the idea and thus a great masterpiece irresistibly rivets your attention until you seem to become actually a part of it. A vacuum is there for you to enter and fill up to the full measure of your æsthetic emotion.

He who had made himself master of the art of living was the Real Man of the Taoist. At birth he enters the realm of dreams only to awaken to reality at death. He tempers his own

---

☐ Jiu-jitsu 柔術　☐ Taoteiking『道徳経』《老子が著した道家の書》　☐ conserve 温存する　☐ beholder 見る人　☐ irresistibly どうしようもないほどに　☐ rivet ～を引きつける　☐ Real Man 真の人間　☐ temper 加減する

brightness in order to merge himself into the obscurity of others. He is "reluctant, as one who crosses a stream in winter; hesitating, as one who fears the neighbourhood; respectful, like a guest; trembling, like ice that is about to melt; unassuming, like a piece of wood not yet carved; vacant, like a valley; formless, like troubled waters." To him the three jewels of life were Pity, Economy, and Modesty.

If now we turn our attention to Zennism we shall find that it emphasises the teachings of Taoism. Zen is a name derived from the Sanscrit word Dhyana, which signifies meditation. It claims that through consecrated meditation may be attained supreme selfrealisation. Meditation is one of the six ways through which Buddhahood may be reached, and the Zen sectarians affirm that Sakyamuni laid special stress on this method in his later teachings, handing down the

□ obscurity 無名の人　□ carve 彫刻をする　□ Modesty 謙譲　□ Sanscrit サンスクリット語　□ Dhyana 禅那《心身が動揺しなくなった状態のこと》　□ consecrate 〜をささげる　□ selfrealisation 自己実現　□ affirm 〜を支持する□ Sakyamuni 釈迦牟尼《仏教の開祖である釈迦の尊称》

rules to his chief disciple Kashiapa. According to their tradition Kashiapa, the first Zen patriarch, imparted the secret to Ananda, who in turn passed it on to successive patriarchs until it reached Bodhi Dharma, the twenty-eighth. Bodhi Dharma came to Northern China in the early half of the sixth century and was the first patriarch of Chinese Zen. There is much uncertainty about the history of these patriarchs and their doctrines. In its philosophical aspect early Zennism seems to have affinity on one hand to the Indian Negativism of Nagarjuna and on the other to the Gnan philosophy formulated by Sanchara-charya. The first teaching of Zen as we know it at the present day must be attributed to the sixth Chinese patriarch Yeno (637–713), founder of Southern Zen, so-called from the fact of its predominance in Southern China. He is closely followed by the great Baso (died 788)

□ Kashiapa 迦葉《釈迦の弟子》　□ patriarch 始祖　□ Ananda 阿難陀《釈迦の弟子》　□ Indian Negativism of Nagarjuna 那伽閼剌樹那のインド否定論　□ Gnan philosophy 無明観　□ Sanchara-charya 商羯羅阿闍梨《700–750頃、中世インドの思想家》　□ attribute 〜をゆえんとする　□ Yeno 慧能《中国唐時代の禅宗僧》　□ predominance 優勢　□ Baso 馬祖《中国唐時代の僧》

who made of Zen a living influence in Celestial life. Hiakujo (719–814), the pupil of Baso, first instituted the Zen monastery and established a ritual and regulations for its government. In the discussions of the Zen school after the time of Baso we find the play of the Yangtse Kiang mind causing an accession of native modes of thought in contrast to the former Indian idealism. Whatever sectarian pride may assert to the contrary, one cannot help being impressed by the similarity of Southern Zen to the teachings of Laotse, and the Taoist Conversationalists. In the Taoteiking we already find allusions to the importance of self-concentration and the need of properly regulating the breath—essential points in the practice of Zen meditation. Some of the best commentaries on the Book of Laotse have been written by Zen scholars.

Zennism, like Taoism, is the worship of

☐ Hiakujo 百丈《中国唐時代の僧》 ☐ accession 増加 ☐ allusion 言及
☐ Book of Laotse 老子（道教）の注釈本

Relativity. One master defines Zen as the art of feeling the polar star in the southern sky. Truth can be reached only through the comprehension of opposites. Again, Zennism, like Taoism, is a strong advocate of individualism. Nothing is real except that which concerns the working of our own minds. Yeno, the sixth patriarch, once saw two monks watching the flag of a pagoda fluttering in the wind. One said "It is the wind that moves," the other said "It is the flag that moves"; but Yeno explained to them that the real movement was neither of the wind nor the flag, but of something within their own minds. Hiakujo was walking in the forest with a disciple when a hare scurried off at their approach. "Why does the hare fly from you?" asked Hiakujo. "Because he is afraid of me," was the answer. "No," said the master, "it is because you have a murderous instinct." This dialogue recalls that of

☐ polar star 北極星　☐ advocate 提唱者　☐ pagoda 仏塔　☐ flutter はためく
☐ hare 野うさぎ　☐ scurry off 慌てて走り去る　☐ murderous 残忍な

Soshi (Chuangtse), the Taoist. One day Soshi was walking on the bank of a river with a friend. "How delightfully the fishes are enjoying themselves in the water!" exclaimed Soshi. His friend spake to him thus: "You are not a fish; how do you know that the fishes are enjoying themselves?" "You are not myself," returned Soshi; "how do you know that I do not know that the fishes are enjoying themselves?"

Zen was often opposed to the precepts of orthodox Buddhism even as Taoism was opposed to Confucianism. To the transcendental insight of the Zen, words were but an incumbrance to thought; the whole sway of Buddhist scriptures only commentaries on personal speculation. The followers of Zen aimed at direct communion with the inner nature of things, regarding their outward accessories only as impediments to a clear perception of Truth.

□ spake SPEAK の過去《古》 □ precept 教え □ transcendental 卓越した
□ incumbrance 妨げ □ sway 支配 □ scripture 経典 □ communion 交感
□ impediment 障害

It was this love of the Abstract that led the Zen to prefer black and white sketches to the elaborately coloured paintings of the classic Buddhist School. Some of the Zen even became iconoclastic as a result of their endeavour to recognise the Buddha in themselves rather than through images and symbolism. We find Tankawosho breaking up a wooden statue of Buddha on a wintry day to make a fire. "What sacrilege!" said the horror-stricken bystander. "I wish to get the Shali out of the ashes," calmly rejoined the Zen. "But you certainly will not get Shali from this image!" was the angry retort, to which Tanka replied, "If I do not, this is certainly not a Buddha and I am committing no sacrilege." Then he turned to warm himself over the kindling fire.

A special contribution of Zen to Eastern thought was its recognition of the mundane as of equal importance with the spiritual. It held

---

□ iconoclastic 偶像破壊主義の □ endeavour 努力 □ Tankawosho 丹霞和尚《?-1119、中国宋時代の僧》 □ wintry 冬の □ sacrilege 冒とく行為 □ horror-stricken ぞっとした □ bystander 近くにいる人 □ Shali 舎利《釈迦の遺骨》 □ retort 反論 □ kindling fire たき火

that in the great relation of things there was no distinction of small and great, an atom possessing equal possibilities with the universe. The seeker for perfection must discover in his own life the reflection of the inner light. The organisation of the Zen monastery was very significant of this point of view. To every member, except the abbot, was assigned some special work in the care-taking of the monastery, and curiously enough, to the novices were committed the lighter duties, while to the most respected and advanced monks were given the more irksome and menial tasks. Such services formed a part of the Zen discipline and every least action must be done absolutely perfectly. Thus many a weighty discussion ensued while weeding the garden, paring a turnip, or serving tea. The whole ideal of Teaism is a result of this Zen conception of greatness in the smallest incidents of life. Taoism

□distinction 区別 □abbot 座主、宗教施設の長 □novice 新参者 □commit 委任する □irksome 厄介な □menial 単調な □ensue 引き続き起こる □weed 雑草を取る □pare 皮をむく □turnip カブ

furnished the basis for æsthetic ideals, Zennism made them practical.

Chapter 4
The Tea-Room

The Tea-Room

The tea-room does not pretend to be other than a mere cottage – The simplicity and purism of the tea-room – Symbolism in the construction of the tea-room – The system of its decoration – A sanctuary from the vexations of the outer world.

*T*o European architects brought up on the traditions of stone and brick construction, our Japanese method of building with wood and bamboo seems scarcely worthy to be ranked as architecture. It is but quite recently that a competent student of Western architecture has recognised and paid tribute to the remarkable perfection of our great temples. Such being the case as regards our classic architecture, we could hardly expect the outsider to appreciate the subtle beauty of the tearoom, its principles of construction and decoration being entirely different from those of the West.

The tea-room (the Sukiya) does not pretend to be other than a mere cottage—a straw hut, as we call it. The original ideographs for Sukiya mean the Abode of Fancy. Latterly the various tea-masters substituted various Chinese characters according to their conception of the

---

□ competent 優秀な　□ tribute 賛辞　□ Sukiya 数寄屋　□ straw hut 藁葺きの小屋　□ Abode of Fancy お好みの家　□ substitute 〜を代わりに使う

tea-room, and the term Sukiya may signify the Abode of Vacancy or the Abode of the Unsymmetrical. It is an Abode of Fancy inasmuch as it is an ephemeral structure built to house a poetic impulse. It is an Abode of Vacancy inasmuch as it is devoid of ornamentation except for what may be placed in it to satisfy some æsthetic need of the moment. It is an Abode of the Unsymmetrical inasmuch as it is consecrated to the worship of the Imperfect, purposely leaving some thing unfinished for the play of the imagination to complete. The ideals of Teaism have since the sixteenth century influenced our architecture to such a degree that the ordinary Japanese interior of the present day, on account of the extreme simplicity and chasteness of its scheme of decoration, appears to foreigners almost barren.

The first independent tea-room was the

□ Abode of Vacancy 空き家　□ Abode of the Unsymmetrical 非対称の家　□ devoid of 〜を欠いている　□ ornamentation 装飾　□ on account of 〜の理由で　□ chasteness 簡素なこと

creation of Senno-Soyeki, commonly known by his later name of Rikiu, the greatest of all tea-masters, who, in the sixteenth century, under the patronage of Taiko-Hideyoshi, instituted and brought to a high state of perfection the formalities of the Tea-ceremony. The proportions of the tearoom had been previously determined by Jowo—a famous tea-master of the fifteenth century. The early tea-room consisted merely of a portion of the ordinary drawing-room partitioned off by screens for the purpose of the tea-gathering. The portion partitioned off was called the Kakoi (enclosure), a name still applied to those tea-rooms which are built into a house and are not independent constructions. The Sukiya consists of the tea-room proper, designed to accommodate not more than five persons, a number suggestive of the saying "more than the Graces and less than the Muses," an

---

□ Senno-Soyeki 千宗易《利休の別名》 □ Rikiu 千利休《1522–1591、安土桃山時代の茶人》 □ patronage 後援 □ Taiko-Hideyoshi 太閤秀吉《豊臣秀吉、1537–1598》 □ institute 制定する □ formality 作法 □ Jowo 紹鴎《1502–1555、室町時代後期の茶人》 □ partitioned 区切られた □ enclosure 囲い □ accommodate 〜を収容できる □ "more than the Graces and less than the Muses,"「グレース（美の三女神）よりは多く、ミューズ（芸術の九女神）よりは少ない」

anteroom (midsuya) where the tea utensils are washed and arranged before being brought in, a portico (machiai) in which the guests wait until they receive the summons to enter the tearoom, and a garden path (the roji) which connects the machiai with the tea-room. The tea-room is unimpressive in appearance. It is smaller than the smallest of Japanese houses, while the materials used in its construction are intended to give the suggestion of refined poverty. Yet we must remember that all this is the result of profound artistic forethought, and that the details have been worked out with care perhaps even greater than that expended on the building of the richest palaces and temples. A good tea-room is more costly than an ordinary mansion, for the selection of its materials, as well as its workmanship, requires immense care and precision. Indeed the carpenters employed by

☐ anteroom (midsuya) 控え室（水屋）　☐ portico (machiai) 玄関ポーチ（待合）
☐ summons 呼び出し　☐ garden path (the roji) 庭園の小道（露地）　☐ refined 洗練された　☐ poverty 貧しさ　☐ profound 深遠な　☐ forethought 考慮
☐ expend ～を費やす　☐ mansion 屋敷　☐ workmanship 職人技
☐ immense 計り知れない　☐ precision 正確さ

the tea-masters form a distinct and highly honoured class among artisans, their work being no less delicate than that of the makers of lacquer cabinets.

The tea-room is not only different from any production of Western architecture, but also contrasts strongly with the classical architecture of Japan itself. Our ancient noble edifices, whether secular or ecclesiastical, were not to be despised even as regards their mere size. The few that have been spared in the disastrous conflagrations of centuries are still capable of aweing us by the grandeur and richness of their decoration. Huge pillars of wood from two to three feet in diameter and from thirty to forty feet high, supported, by a complicated network of brackets, the enormous beams which groaned under the weight of the tile-covered slanting roofs. The material and mode of construction, though weak against

☐ artisan 職人 ☐ lacquer うるし ☐ edifice 大建築物 ☐ secular 俗人の
☐ ecclesiastical 教会の ☐ despise 軽視する ☐ conflagration 大火災 ☐ awe
～を畏怖させる ☐ grandeur 壮麗さ ☐ groan きしむ

fire, proved itself strong against earthquakes, and was well suited to the climatic conditions of the country. In the Golden Hall of Horiuji and the Pagoda of Yakushiji, we have noteworthy examples of the durability of our wooden architecture. These buildings have practically stood intact for nearly twelve centuries. The interior of the old temples and palaces was profusely decorated. In the Hoodo temple at Uji, dating from the tenth century, we can still see the elaborate canopy and gilded baldachinos, many-coloured and inlaid with mirrors and mother-of-pearl, as well as remains of the paintings and sculpture which formerly covered the walls. Later, at Nikko and in the Nijo castle in Kyoto, we see structural beauty sacrificed to a wealth of ornamentation which in colour and exquisite detail equals the utmost gorgeousness of Arabian or Moorish effort.

□ Golden Hall of Horiuji 法隆寺の金堂　□ Pagoda of Yakushiji 薬師寺の仏塔　□ noteworthy 特筆すべき　□ durability 耐久性　□ intact 完全なままの　□ profusely 豊富に　□ elaborate 精巧な　□ canopy 天蓋（仏像などをおおう装飾）　□ gilded 金箔を貼った　□ baldachino 天蓋　□ inlaid（宝石などが）ちりばめられた　□ mother-of-pearl（貝の内側の）真珠層　□ exquisite 精緻な　□ utmost 最高の　□ Moorish ムーア様式の（13–16世紀にスペインを征服したイスラム教徒）

The simplicity and purism of the tea-room resulted from emulation of the Zen monastery. A Zen monastery differs from those of other Buddhist sects inasmuch as it is meant only to be a dwelling place for the monks. Its chapel is not a place of worship or pilgrimage, but a college room where the students congregate for discussion and the practice of meditation. The room is bare except for a central alcove in which, behind the altar, is a statue of Bodhi Dharma, the founder of the sect, or of Sakyamuni attended by Kashiapa and Ananda, the two earliest Zen patriarchs. On the altar, flowers and incense are offered up in memory of the great contributions which these sages made to Zen. We have already said that it was the ritual instituted by the Zen monks of successively drinking tea out of a bowl before the image of Bodhi Dharma, which laid the foundations of

□ emulation 模倣　□ monastery 僧院　□ pilgrimage 参詣　□ congregate 集会　□ alcove 壁のくぼみ

the tea-ceremony. We might add here that the altar of the Zen chapel was the prototype of the Tokonoma,—the place of honour in a Japanese room where paintings and flowers are placed for the edification of the guests.

All our great tea-masters were students of Zen and attempted to introduce the spirit of Zennism into the actualities of life. Thus the room, like the other equipments of the tea-ceremony, reflects many of the Zen doctrines.

The size of the orthodox tea-room, which is four mats and a half, or ten feet square, is determined by a passage in the Sutra of Vikramadytia. In that interesting work, Vikramadytia welcomes the Saint Manjushiri and eighty-four thousand disciples of Buddha in a room of this size,—an allegory based on the theory of the non-existence of space to the truly enlightened. Again the roji, the garden path which leads

---

□ altar 祭壇　□ edification 教化　□ actuality 現実性　□ Sutra 経典　□ Vikramadytia ヴィマラキールティ《古代インドの商人、釈迦の弟子》　□ Saint Manjushiri 文殊師利菩薩《智慧を司る仏》　□ enlightened 悟りを開いた

from the machiai to the tea-room, signified the first stage of meditation,—the passage into self-illumination. The roji was intended to break connection with the outside world, and to produce a fresh sensation conducive to the full enjoyment of æstheticism in the tea-room itself. One who has trodden this garden path cannot fail to remember how his spirit, as he walked in the twilight of evergreens over the regular irregularities of the stepping stones, beneath which lay dried pine needles, and passed beside the moss-covered granite lanterns, became uplifted above ordinary thoughts. One may be in the midst of a city, and yet feel as if he were in the forest far away from the dust and din of civilisation. Great was the ingenuity displayed by the tea-masters in producing these effects of serenity and purity. The nature of the sensations to be aroused in passing through the roji differed with

□ self-illumination 自己啓蒙　□ trodden TREAD（〜を歩く）の過去分詞
□ granite 御影石　□ ingenuity 創意あふれる構想　□ serenity 静穏

different tea-masters. Some, like Rikiu, aimed at utter loneliness, and claimed the secret of making a roji was contained in the ancient ditty:

> *I looked beyond;*
> *Flowers are not,*
> *Nor tinted leaves.*
> *On the sea beach*
> *A solitary cottage stands*
> *In the waning light*
> *Of an autumn eve.*

Others, like Kobori-Enshiu, sought for a different effect. Enshiu said the idea of the garden path was to be found in the following verses:

> *A cluster of summer trees,*
> *A bit of the sea,*
> *A pale evening moon.*

□ ditty 歌　□ waning 徐々に弱まる　□ Kobori-Enshiu 小堀遠州《1579–1647、近江小室藩藩主、茶人》　□ verse 詩　□ cluster 一群

It is not difficult to gather his meaning. He wished to create the attitude of a newly-awakened soul still lingering amid shadowy dreams of the past, yet bathing in the sweet unconsciousness of a mellow spiritual light, and yearning for the freedom that lay in the expanse beyond.

Thus prepared the guest will silently approach the sanctuary, and, if a samurai, will leave his sword on the rack beneath the eaves, the tea-room being preeminently the house of peace. Then he will bend low and creep into the room through a small door not more than three feet in height. This proceeding was incumbent on all guests, —high and low alike,—and was intended to inculcate humility. The order of precedence having been mutually agreed upon while resting in the machiai, the guests one by one will enter noiselessly and take their seats, first making obeisance to the picture or flower arrangement

☐ mellow 柔らかい ☐ yearning 憧れ ☐ expanse 天空 ☐ sanctuary 神聖な場所 ☐ eave 軒、ひさし ☐ preeminently 卓越して ☐ creep 四つんばいで進む ☐ proceeding 手順 ☐ incumbent 行う義務のある ☐ humility 謙虚 ☐ precedence 優先権 ☐ obeisance 敬意

on the tokonoma. The host will not enter the room until all the guests have seated themselves and quiet reigns with nothing to break the silence save the note of the boiling water in the iron kettle. The kettle sings well, for pieces of iron are so arranged in the bottom as to produce a peculiar melody in which one may hear the echoes of a cataract muffled by clouds, of a distant sea breaking among the rocks, a rainstorm sweeping through a bamboo forest, or of the soughing of pines on some faraway hill.

Even in the daytime the light in the room is subdued, for the low eaves of the slanting roof admit but few of the sun's rays. Everything is sober in tint from the ceiling to the floor; the guests themselves have carefully chosen garments of unobtrusive colours. The mellowness of age is over all, everything suggestive of recent acquirement being tabooed save only the one note of contrast furnished by the bamboo dipper and the linen napkin, both immaculately white and new. However faded the tea-room and the tea-equipage may seem, everything is absolutely clean. Not a particle of dust will be found in the darkest corner, for if any exists the host is not a tea-master. One of the first requisites of a tea-master is the knowledge of how to sweep, clean, and wash, for there is an art in cleaning and dusting. A piece of antique metal work must not be attacked with the unscrupulous zeal of the Dutch housewife. Dripping water from a flower vase need not be wiped away, for it may be suggestive of dew and coolness.

In this connection there is a story of Rikiu which well illustrates the ideas of cleanliness entertained by the tea-masters. Rikiu was watching his son Shoan as he swept and watered the garden path. "Not clean enough," said Rikiu,

☐ dipper ひしゃく　☐ linen 麻布　☐ particle ちり　☐ requisite 必要条件
☐ dusting ほこり取り　☐ unscrupulous 思慮のない　☐ zeal 熱意　☐ Shoan 小庵《1546–1614、利休の娘婿、茶人》

when Shoan had finished his task, and bade him try again. After a weary hour the son turned to Rikiu: "Father, there is nothing more to be done. The steps have been washed for the third time, the stone lanterns and the trees are well sprinkled with water, moss and lichens are shining with a fresh verdure; not a twig, not a leaf have I left on the ground." "Young fool," chided the tea-master, "that is not the way a garden path should be swept." Saying this, Rikiu stepped into the garden, shook a tree and scattered over the garden gold and crimson leaves, scraps of the brocade of autumn! What Rikiu demanded was not cleanliness alone, but the beautiful and the natural also.

The name, Abode of Fancy, implies a structure created to meet some individual artistic requirement. The tea-room is made for the tea-master not the tea-master for the tea-room.

□ bade BID（〜を命じる）の過去《古》 □ weary 疲れた □ lichen 地衣類《苔に似た菌類》 □ verdure 新緑 □ chide たしなめる □ scrap 一片

It is not intended for posterity and is therefore ephemeral. The idea that everyone should have a house of his own is based on an ancient custom of the Japanese race, Shinto superstition ordaining that every dwelling should be evacuated on the death of its chief occupant. Perhaps there may have been some unrealised sanitary reason for this practice. Another early custom was that a newly built house should be provided for each couple that married. It is on account of such customs that we find the Imperial capitals so frequently removed from one site to another in ancient days. The rebuilding, every twenty years, of Ise Temple, the supreme shrine of the Sun-Goddess, is an example of one of these ancient rites which still obtain at the present day. The observance of these customs was only possible with some such form of construction as that furnished by our system of wooden architecture,

---

☐ posterity 後世の人々　☐ ephemeral つかの間の　☐ superstition 迷信
☐ ordain 〜と定める　☐ evacuate 立ち退かせる　☐ occupant 居住者
☐ sanitary 衛生上の　☐ Imperial capital 皇都　☐ rite 儀式

easily pulled down, easily built up. A more lasting style, employing brick and stone, would have rendered migrations impracticable, as indeed they became when the more stable and massive wooden construction of China was adopted by us after the Nara period.

With the predominance of Zen individualism in the fifteenth century, however, the old idea became imbued with a deeper significance as conceived in connection with the tea-room. Zennism, with the Buddhist theory of evanescence and its demands for the mastery of spirit over matter, recognised the house only as a temporary refuge for the body. The body itself was but as a hut in the wilderness, a flimsy shelter made by tying together the grasses that grew around,—when these ceased to be bound together they again became resolved into the original waste. In the tea-room fugitiveness is suggested in the thatched roof, frailty in the slender pillars, lightness in the bamboo support, apparent carelessness in the use of commonplace materials. The eternal is to be found only in the spirit which, embodied in these simple surroundings, beautifies them with the subtle light of its refinement.

That the tea-room should be built to suit some individual taste is an enforcement of the principle of vitality in art. Art, to be fully appreciated, must be true to contemporaneous life. It is not that we should ignore the claims of posterity, but that we should seek to enjoy the present more. It is not that we should disregard the creations of the past, but that we should try to assimilate them into our consciousness. Slavish conformity to traditions and formulas fetters the expression of individuality in architecture. We can but weep over those senseless imitations

---

□ thatched roof 茅葺き屋根　□ frailty 弱々しさ　□ contemporaneous 同時代の　□ assimilate 〜を吸収する　□ slavish 奴隷のような　□ conformity 服従　□ fetter 〜に足かせをはめる　□ weep over 〜を嘆き悲しむ

of European buildings which one beholds in modern Japan. We marvel why, among the most progressive Western nations, architecture should be so devoid of originality, so replete with repetitions of obsolete styles. Perhaps we are now passing through an age of democratisation in art, while awaiting the rise of some princely master who shall establish a new dynasty. Would that we loved the ancients more and copied them less! It has been said that the Greeks were great because they never drew from the antique.

The term, Abode of Vacancy, besides conveying the Taoist theory of the all-containing, involves the conception of a continued need of change in decorative motives. The tea-room is absolutely empty, except for what may be placed there temporarily to satisfy some æsthetic mood. Some special art object is brought in for the occasion, and everything else is selected and arranged to enhance the beauty of the principal theme. One cannot listen to different pieces of music at the same time, a real comprehension of the beautiful being possible only through concentration upon some central motive. Thus it will be seen that the system of decoration in our tea-rooms is opposed to that which obtains in the West, where the interior of a house is often converted into a museum. To a Japanese, accustomed to simplicity of ornamentation and frequent change of decorative method, a Western interior permanently filled with a vast array of pictures, statuary, and bric-a-brac gives the impression of mere vulgar display of riches. It calls for a mighty wealth of appreciation to enjoy the constant sight of even a masterpiece, and limitless indeed must be the capacity for artistic feeling in those who can exist day after day in the midst of such confusion

□ principal 第一の　□ array 整列　□ statuary 彫像　□ bric-a-brac 骨董品

of colour and form as is to be often seen in the homes of Europe and America.

The "Abode of the Unsymmetrical" suggests another phase of our decorative scheme. The absence of symmetry in Japanese art objects has been often commented on by Western critics. This, also, is a result of a working out through Zennism of Taoist ideals. Confucianism, with its deep-seated idea of dualism, and Northern Buddhism with its worship of a trinity, were in no way opposed to the expression of symmetry. As a matter of fact, if we study the ancient bronzes of China or the religious arts of the Tang dynasty and the Nara period, we shall recognise a constant striving after symmetry. The decoration of our classical interiors was decidedly regular in its arrangement. The Taoist and Zen conception of perfection, however, was different. The dynamic nature of their philosophy laid more stress upon

☐ symmetry 対称性　☐ critic 評論家　☐ deep-seated 深く根ざした
☐ worship of a trinity 三尊崇拝《中央の中尊の左右に脇侍をおき崇拝すること》
☐ strive 努力する

the process through which perfection was sought than upon perfection itself. True beauty could be discovered only by one who mentally completed the incomplete. The virility of life and art lay in its possibilities for growth. In the tea-room it is left for each guest in imagination to complete the total effect in relation to himself. Since Zennism has become the prevailing mode of thought, the art of the extreme Orient has purposely avoided the symmetrical as expressing not only completion, but repetition. Uniformity of design was considered as fatal to the freshness of imagination. Thus, landscapes, birds, and flowers became the favourite subjects for depiction rather than the human figure, the latter being present in the person of the beholder himself. We are often too much in evidence as it is, and in spite of our vanity even self-regard is apt to become monotonous.

☐ extreme Orient 極東 ☐ repetition 反復 ☐ uniformity 画一性 ☐ fatal 致命的な ☐ depiction 描写 ☐ self-regard 自己愛 ☐ monotonous 単調な

In the tea-room the fear of repetition is a constant presence. The various objects for the decoration of a room should be so selected that no colour or design shall be repeated. If you have a living flower, a painting of flowers is not allowable. If you are using a round kettle, the water pitcher should be angular. A cup with a black glaze should not be associated with a tea-caddy of black lacquer. In placing a vase or an incense burner on the tokonoma, care should be taken not to put it in the exact centre, lest it divide the space into equal halves. The pillar of the tokonoma should be of a different kind of wood from the other pillars, in order to break any suggestion of monotony in the room.

Here again the Japanese method of interior decoration differs from that of the Occident, where we see objects arrayed symmetrically on mantelpieces and elsewhere. In Western houses

☐ allowable 許容できる　☐ water pitcher 水差し　☐ angular 角のある
☐ tea-caddy 棗、茶入　☐ vase 花瓶　☐ incense burner 香炉　☐ Occident 西洋　☐ mantelpieces 暖炉棚

we are often confronted with what appears to us useless reiteration. We find it trying to talk to a man while his full-length portrait stares at us from behind his back We wonder which is real, he of the picture or he who talks, and feel a curious conviction that one of them must be fraud. Many a time have we sat at a festive board contemplating, with a secret shock to our digestion, the representation of abundance on the dining-room walls. Why these pictured victims of chase and sport, the elaborate carvings of fishes and fruit? Why the display of family plates, reminding us of those who have dined and are dead?

The simplicity of the tea-room and its freedom from vulgarity make it truly a sanctuary from the vexations of the outer world. There and there alone can one consecrate himself to undisturbed adoration of the beautiful. In the sixteenth century the tea-room afforded a welcome respite from labour to the fierce warriors and statesmen engaged in the unification and reconstruction of Japan. In the seventeenth century, after the strict formalism of the Tokugawa rule had been developed, it offered the only opportunity possible for the free communion of artistic spirits. Before a great work of art there was no distinction between daimyo, samurai, and commoner. Nowadays industrialism is making true refinement more and more difficult all the world over. Do we not need the tea-room more than ever?

☐ afford 〜を提供する　☐ respite 小休止　☐ fierce 勇猛な　☐ statesman 指導的政治家　☐ formalism 極端な　☐ commoner 平民　☐ industrialism 産業主義

Chapter 5
Art Appreciation

Art Appreciation

Sympathetic communion of minds necessary for art appreciation — The secret understanding between the master and ourselves — The value of suggestion — Art is of value only to the extent that it speaks to us — No real feeling in much of the apparent enthusiasm to-day — Confusion of art with archaeology — We are destroying art in destroying the beautiful in life.

*H*ave you heard the Taoist tale of the Taming of the Harp?

Once in the hoary ages in the Ravine of Lungmen stood a Kiri tree, a veritable king of the forest. It reared its head to talk to the stars; its roots struck deep into the earth, mingling their bronzed coils with those of the silver dragon that slept beneath. And it came to pass that a mighty wizard made of this tree a wondrous harp, whose stubborn spirit should be tamed but by the greatest of musicians. For long the instrument was treasured by the Emperor of China, but all in vain were the efforts of those who in turn tried to draw melody from its strings. In response to their utmost strivings there came from the harp but harsh notes of disdain, ill-according with the songs they fain would sing. The harp refused to recognise a master.

□ Taming of the Harp 『琴慣らし』《道教徒の物語》　□ hoary 年老いた
□ Ravine of Lungmen 竜門の谷《中国洛陽にある地名》　□ Kiri tree 桐の木
□ veritable 真の　□ mingle 〜と絡み合う　□ wondrous おどろくべき
□ stubborn 強情な　□ treasure 〜を大切に保管する　□ note 音　□ disdain 蔑視　□ ill-according 不協和音

At last came Peiwoh, the prince of harpists. With tender hand he caressed the harp as one might seek to soothe an unruly horse, and softly touched the chords. He sang of nature and the seasons, of high mountains and flowing waters, and all the memories of the tree awoke! Once more the sweet breath of spring played amidst its branches. The young cataracts, as they danced down the ravine, laughed to the budding flowers. Anon were heard the dreamy voices of summer with its myriad insects, the gentle pattering of rain, the wail of the cuckoo. Hark! a tiger roars,—the valley answers again. It is autumn; in the desert night, sharp like a sword gleams the moon upon the frosted grass. Now winter reigns, and through the snow-filled air swirl flocks of swans and rattling hailstones beat upon the boughs with fierce delight.

Then Peiwoh changed the key and sang of

☐ Peiwoh 伯牙《中国春秋時代の琴の名手》 ☐ caress 〜をなでる ☐ soothe 〜をなだめる ☐ Anon すぐに ☐ myriad 無数の ☐ patter パタパタと音を立てる ☐ wail 嘆き悲しむ声 ☐ cuckoo カッコウ《鳥》 ☐ hark 耳を傾ける ☐ swirl 旋回する ☐ flock of 〜の群れ ☐ rattling カタカタと音を立てる ☐ hailstones ヒョウ、あられ ☐ bough 大きな枝

love. The forest swayed like an ardent swain deep lost in thought. On high, like a haughty maiden, swept a cloud bright and fair; but passing, trailed long shadows on the ground, black like despair. Again the mode was changed; Peiwoh sang of war, of clashing steel and trampling steeds. And in the harp arose the tempest of Lungmen, the dragon rode the lightning, the thundering avalanche crashed through the hills. In ecstacy the Celestial monarch asked Peiwoh wherein lay the secret of his victory. "Sire," he replied, "others have failed because they sang but of themselves. I left the harp to choose its theme, and knew not truly whether the harp had been Peiwoh or Peiwoh were the harp."

This story well illustrates the mystery of art appreciation. The masterpiece is a symphony played upon our finest feelings. True art is Peiwoh, and we the harp of Lungmen. At the

---

□ ardent 情熱的な □ swain （男の）恋人 □ haughty お高くとまった
□ trample ずかずか歩く □ steed 馬《古》 □ avalanche 雪崩 □ sire 陛下《古》

magic touch of the beautiful the secret chords of our being are awakened, we vibrate and thrill in response to its call. Mind speaks to mind. We listen to the unspoken, we gaze upon the unseen. The master calls forth notes we know not of. Memories long forgotten all come back to us with a new significance. Hopes stifled by fear, yearnings that we dare not recognise, stand forth in new glory. Our mind is the canvas on which the artists lay their colour; their pigments are our emotions; their chiaroscuro the light of joy, the shadow of sadness. The masterpiece is of ourselves, as we are of the masterpiece.

The sympathetic communion of minds necessary for art appreciation must be based on mutual concession. The spectator must cultivate the proper attitude for receiving the message, as the artist must know to impart it. The tea-master, Kobori-Enshiu, himself a daimyo, has left

□vibrate 振動する　□call forth 〜を呼び起こす　□significance 意味　□stifle 〜を抑えつける　□pigment 絵の具　□chiaroscuro 明暗の配合　□concession 譲歩　□cultivate 〜を養成する

to us these memorable words: "Approach a great painting as thou wouldst approach a great prince." In order to understand a masterpiece, you must lay yourself low before it and await with bated breath its least utterance. An eminent Sung critic once made a charming confession. Said he: "In my young days I praised the master whose pictures I liked, but as my judgment matured I praised myself for liking what the masters had chosen to have me like." It is to be deplored that so few of us really take pains to study the moods of the masters. In our stubborn ignorance we refuse to render them this simple courtesy, and thus often miss the rich repast of beauty spread before our very eyes. A master has always something to offer, while we go hungry solely because of our own lack of appreciation.

To the sympathetic a masterpiece becomes a living reality towards which we feel drawn in

---

□ memorable 印象的な □ thou 汝《YOUの古語》 □ wouldst WILL の二人称単数過去《古》 □ bate 減らす《古》 □ utterance 発言 □ confession 告白
□ mature 成熟する □ deplore ～を遺憾に思う □ ignorance 無知
□ courtesy 礼儀 □ repast ごちそう

bonds of comradeship. The masters are immortal, for their loves and fears live in us over and over again. It is rather the soul than the hand, the man than the technique, which appeals to us,—the more human the call the deeper is our response. It is because of this secret understanding between the master and ourselves that in poetry or romance we suffer and rejoice with the hero and heroine. Chikamatsu, our Japanese Shakespeare, has laid down as one of the first principles of dramatic composition the importance of taking the audience into the confidence of the author. Several of his pupils submitted plays for his approval, but only one of the pieces appealed to him. It was a play somewhat resembling the Comedy of Errors, in which twin brethren suffer through mistaken identity. "This," said Chikamatsu, "has the proper spirit of the drama, for it takes the audience into

□ comradeship 友達関係　□ immortal 不滅の　□ rejoice 喜ぶ
□ Chikamatsu 近松門左衛門《1653-1725、江戸中期の浄瑠璃・歌舞伎脚本作家》
□ composition 構成　□ submit 〜を提出する　□ Comedy of Errors『間違いの喜劇』《1594年、シェイクスピア作の戯曲》　□ brethren 兄弟《古》

consideration. The public is permitted to know more than the actors. It knows where the mistake lies, and pities the poor figures on the board who innocently rush to their fate."

The great masters both of the East and the West never forgot the value of suggestion as a means for taking the spectator into their confidence. Who can contemplate a masterpiece without being awed by the immense vista of thought presented to our consideration? How familiar and sympathetic are they all; how cold in contrast the modern commonplaces! In the former we feel the warm outpouring of a man's heart; in the latter only a formal salute. Engrossed in his technique, the modern rarely rises above himself. Like the musicians who vainly invoked the Lungmen harp, he sings only of himself. His works may be nearer science, but are further from humanity. We have an old

□ permit 可能にする　□ pity 〜に同情する　□ vista 展望　□ outpouring ほとばしり　□ salute 挨拶　□ engrossed in 〜に没頭する　□ vainly 無駄に　□ invoke 〜を呼び覚ます

saying in Japan that a woman cannot love a man who is truly vain, for there is no crevice in his heart for love to enter and fill up. In art vanity is equally fatal to sympathetic feeling, whether on the part of the artist or the public.

Nothing is more hallowing than the union of kindred spirits in art. At the moment of meeting, the art lover transcends himself. At once he is and is not. He catches a glimpse of Infinity, but words cannot voice his delight, for the eye has no tongue. Freed from the fetters of matter, his spirit moves in the rhythm of things. It is thus that art becomes akin to religion and ennobles mankind. It is this which makes a masterpiece something sacred. In the old days the veneration in which the Japanese held the work of the great artist was intense. The tea-masters guarded their treasures with religious secrecy, and it was often necessary to open a whole series

---

□ hallowing 尊い　□ kindred 同類の　□ transcend 〜を超越する　□ glimpse 〜を垣間見る　□ akin to 〜と同種である　□ sacred 神聖な　□ veneration 畏敬の念

of boxes, one within another, before reaching the shrine itself—the silken wrapping within whose soft folds lay the holy of holies. Rarely was the object exposed to view, and then only to the initiated.

At the time when Teaism was in the ascendency the Taiko's generals would be better satisfied with the present of a rare work of art than a large grant of territory as a reward of victory. Many of our favourite dramas are based on the loss and recovery of a noted masterpiece. For instance, in one play the palace of Lord Hosokawa, in which was preserved the celebrated painting of Dharuma by Sesson, suddenly takes fire through the negligence of the samurai in charge. Resolved at all hazards to rescue the precious painting, he rushes into the burning building and seizes the kakemono, only to find all means of exit cut off by the flames.

☐ silken 絹織りの　☐ holy of holies 聖域　☐ initiate 〜に新規入会させる
☐ ascendency 優勢　☐ Lord Hosokawa 細川氏《江戸時代初期の大名、細川幽斎》
☐ at all hazards どんな危険を冒しても　☐ seize 〜を掴む

Thinking only of the picture, he slashes open his body with his sword, wraps his torn sleeve about the Sesson, and plunges it into the gaping wound. The fire is at last extinguished. Among the smoking embers is found a half-consumed corpse, within which reposes the treasure un-injured by the fire. Horrible as such tales are, they illustrate the great value that we set upon a masterpiece, as well as the devotion of a trusted samurai.

We must remember, however, that art is of value only to the extent that it speaks to us. It might be a universal language if we ourselves were universal in our sympathies. Our finite nature, the power of tradition and conventionality, as well as our hereditary instincts, restrict the scope of our capacity for artistic enjoyment. Our very individuality establishes in one sense a limit to our understanding; and our æsthetic

□ plunge ～を押し込む　□ gaping パックリと割れた　□ extinguish 消す　□ ember 燃えさし　□ half-consumed 生焼けの　□ corpse 死体　□ repose ～を託す　□ finite 限界のある　□ conventionality 因習　□ restrict ～を制限する

personality seeks its own affinities in the creations of the past. It is true that with cultivation our sense of art appreciation broadens, and we become able to enjoy many hitherto unrecognised expressions of beauty. But, after all, we see only our own image in the universe,—our particular idiosyncrasies dictate the mode of our perceptions. The tea-masters collected only objects which fell strictly within the measure of their individual appreciation.

One is reminded in this connection of a story concerning Kobori-Enshiu. Enshiu was complimented by his disciples on the admirable taste he had displayed in the choice of his collection. Said they, "Each piece is such that no one could help admiring. It shows that you had better taste than had Rikiu, for his collection could only be appreciated by one beholder in a thousand." Sorrowfully Enshiu replied: "This only proves

□ cultivation 養成　□ hitherto これまでは　□ dictate 〜を決定づける
□ perception 感じ方　□ sorrowfully 悲しげに

how commonplace I am. The great Rikiu dared to love only those objects which personally appealed to him, whereas I unconsciously cater to the taste of the majority. Verily, Rikiu was one in a thousand among tea-masters."

It is much to be regretted that so much of the apparent enthusiasm for art at the present day has no foundation in real feeling. In this democratic age of ours men clamour for what is popularly considered the best, regardless of their feelings. They want the costly, not the refined; the fashionable, not the beautiful. To the masses, contemplation of illustrated periodicals, the worthy product of their own industrialism, would give more digestible food for artistic enjoyment than the early Italians or the Ashikaga masters, whom they pretend to admire. The name of the artist is more important to them than the quality of the work. As a Chinese critic complained many centuries ago, "People criticise a picture by their ear." It is this lack of genuine appreciation that is responsible for the pseudo-classic horrors that today greet us wherever we turn.

Another common mistake is that of confusing art with archaeology. The veneration born of antiquity is one of the best traits in the human character, and fain would we have it cultivated to a greater extent. The old masters are rightly to be honoured for opening the path to future enlightenment. The mere fact that they have passed unscathed through centuries of criticism and come down to us still covered with glory commands our respect. But we should be foolish indeed if we valued their achievement simply on the score of age. Yet we allow our historical sympathy to override our æsthetic discrimination. We offer flowers of approbation when the artist is safely laid in his grave. The nineteenth century,

☐ pseudo-classic 偽古典の ☐ archaeology 考古学 ☐ antiquity 古いもの
☐ enlightenment 文明の開化 ☐ unscathed 無傷で ☐ override 〜を踏みにじる ☐ discrimination 識別(力) ☐ approbation 称賛

pregnant with the theory of evolution, has moreover created in us the habit of losing sight of the individual in the species. A collector is anxious to acquire specimens to illustrate a period or a school, and forgets that a single masterpiece can teach us more than any number of the mediocre products of a given period or school. We classify too much and enjoy too little. The sacrifice of the æsthetic to the so-called scientific method of exhibition has been the bane of many museums.

The claims of contemporary art cannot be ignored in any vital scheme of life. The art of today is that which really belongs to us: it is our own reflection. In condemning it we but condemn ourselves. We say that the present age possesses no art:—who is responsible for this? It is indeed a shame that despite all our rhapsodies about the ancients we pay so little attention to our own possibilities. Struggling artists, weary

□ pregnant 〜で満ちた　□ specimen 見本　□ mediocre 二流の　□ classify 〜を分類する　□ bane 悩みの種　□ vital 生きるための　□ scheme 構想
□ rhapsody 熱狂的な言葉

souls lingering in the shadow of cold disdain! In our self-centred century, what inspiration do we offer them? The past may well look with pity at the poverty of our civilisation; the future will laugh at the barrenness of our art. We are destroying art in destroying the beautiful in life. Would that some great wizard might from the stem of society shape a mighty harp whose strings would resound to the touch of genius.

□ inspiration 創造性を刺激するもの　□ barrenness 不毛　□ resound 鳴り響く

Chapter 6
Flowers

Flowers

Flowers our constant friends — The Master of Flowers — The waste of Flowers among Western communities — The art of floriculture in the East — The Tea-Masters and the Cult of Flowers — The Art of Flower Arrangement — The adoration of the Flower for its own sake — The Flower-Masters — Two main branches of the schools of Flower Arrangement, the Formalistic and the Naturalesque.

*I*n the trembling grey of a spring dawn, when the birds were whispering in mysterious cadence among the trees, have you not felt that they were talking to their mates about the flowers? Surely with mankind the appreciation of flowers must have been coeval with the poetry of love. Where better than in a flower, sweet in its unconsciousness, fragrant because of its silence, can we image the unfolding of a virgin soul? The primeval man in offering the first garland to his maiden thereby transcended the brute. He became human in thus rising above the crude necessities of nature. He entered the realm of art when he perceived the subtle use of the useless.

In joy or sadness, flowers are our constant friends. We eat, drink, sing, dance, and flirt with them. We wed and christen with flowers. We dare not die without them. We have worshipped with the lily, we have meditated with the lotus,

---

☐ cadence リズム ☐ coeval with 〜と同時代に ☐ fragrant かぐわしい
☐ primeval 原始時代の ☐ garland 花冠 ☐ brute けだものの ☐ flirt 戯れる
☐ christen 〜に命名する ☐ meditate 瞑想する

we have charged in battle array with the rose and the chrysanthemum. We have even attempted to speak in the language of flowers. How could we live without them? It frightens one to conceive of a world bereft of their presence. What solace do they not bring to the bedside of the sick. What a light of bliss to the darkness of weary spirits? Their serene tenderness restores to us our waning confidence in the universe even as the intent gaze of a beautiful child recalls our lost hopes. When we are laid low in the dust it is they who linger in sorrow over our graves.

Sad as it is, we cannot conceal the fact that in spite of our companionship with flowers we have not risen very far above the brute. Scratch the sheepskin and the wolf within us will soon show his teeth. It has been said that man at ten is an animal, at twenty a lunatic, at thirty a failure, at forty a fraud, and at fifty a criminal. Perhaps he

□battle array 戦闘隊形　□chrysanthemum 菊　□bereft BEREAVE（奪い去る）の過去・過去分詞　□solace 慰め　□bliss 至福　□restore 〜を回復させる　□companionship 親交　□lunatic 狂人

becomes a criminal because he has never ceased to be an animal. Nothing is real to us but hunger, nothing sacred except our own desires. Shrine after shrine has crumbled before our eyes; but one altar forever is preserved, that whereon we burn incense to the supreme idol,—ourselves. Our god is great, and money is his Prophet! We devastate nature in order to make sacrifice to him. We boast that we have conquered Matter and forget that it is Matter that has enslaved us. What atrocities do we not perpetrate in the name of culture and refinement!

Tell me, gentle flowers, teardrops of the stars, standing in the garden, nodding your heads to the bees as they sing of the dews and the sunbeams, are you aware of the fearful doom that awaits you? Dream on, sway and frolic while you may in the gentle breezes of summer. Tomorrow a ruthless hand will close around your throats.

□ crumble 崩れ落ちる　□ whereon そのうえに〜するもの《古語の関係副詞》
□ prophet 予言者　□ devastate 〜を破壊する　□ enslave 〜を奴隷にする
□ atrocity 残虐行為　□ perpetrate しでかす　□ teardrop 涙の粒　□ dew 露
□ doom 悲運　□ frolic 浮かれ騒ぐ　□ ruthless 無慈悲な

You will be wrenched, torn asunder limb by limb, and borne away from your quiet homes. The wretch, she may be passing fair. She may say how lovely you are while her fingers are still moist with your blood. Tell me, will this be kindness? It may be your fate to be imprisoned in the hair of one whom you know to be heartless or to be thrust into the buttonhole of one who would not dare to look you in the face were you a man. It may even be your lot to be confined in some narrow vessel with only stagnant water to quench the maddening thirst that warns of ebbing life.

Flowers, if you were in the land of the Mikado, you might some time meet a dread personage armed with scissors and a tiny saw.

He would call himself a Master of Flowers. He would claim the rights of a doctor and you would instinctively hate him, for you know a doctor always seeks to prolong the troubles of his victims. He would cut, bend, and twist you into those impossible positions which he thinks it proper that you should assume. He would contort your muscles and dislocate your bones like any osteopath. He would burn you with red-hot coals to stop your bleeding, and thrust wires into you to assist your circulation. He would diet you with salt, vinegar, alum, and sometimes, vitriol. Boiling water would be poured on your feet when you seemed ready to faint. It would be his boast that he could keep life within you for two or more weeks longer than would have been possible without his treatment. Would you not have preferred to have been killed at once when you were first captured? What were the crimes you must have committed during your past incarnation to warrant such punishment as this?

The wanton waste of flowers among Western

□ prolong（期間などを）引き伸ばす　□ contort 〜をねじ曲げる　□ dislocate 関節をはずす　□ osteopath 整体師　□ circulation 血液循環　□ alum ミョウバン《化学物質》　□ vitriol 硫酸　□ boast 自慢話　□ past incarnation 前世の姿　□ warrant 〜の正当な理由となる　□ wanton 過剰な

CHAPTER 6　FLOWERS　127

communities is even more appalling than the way they are treated by Eastern Flower-Masters. The number of flowers cut daily to adorn the ballrooms and banquet tables of Europe and America, to be thrown away on the morrow, must be something enormous; if strung together they might garland a continent. Beside this utter carelessness of life, the guilt of the Flower-Master becomes insignificant. He, at least, respects the economy of nature, selects his victims with careful foresight, and after death does honour to their remains. In the West the display of flowers seems to be a part of the pageantry of wealth,— the fancy of a moment. Whither do they all go, these flowers, when the revelry is over? Nothing is more pitiful than to see a faded flower remorselessly flung upon a dung heap.

Why were the flowers born so beautiful and yet so hapless? Insects can sting, and even the meekest of beasts will fight when brought to bay. The bird whose plumage is sought to deck some bonnet can fly from its pursuer, the furred animal whose coat you covet for your own may hide at your approach. Alas! The only flower known to have wings is the butterfly; all others stand helpless before the destroyer. If they shriek in their death agony their cry never reaches our hardened ears. We are ever brutal to those who love and serve us in silence, but the time may come when, for our cruelty, we shall be deserted by these best friends of ours. Have you not noticed that the wild flowers are becoming scarcer every year? It may be that their wise men have told them to depart till man becomes more human. Perhaps they have migrated to heaven.

Much may be said in favour of him who cultivates plants. The man of the pot is far more humane than he of the scissors. We watch with

□meek おとなしい　□plumage 羽毛　□pursuer 追っ手　□furred 毛皮をまとった　□covet for 〜を欲しがる　□alas ああ悲しいかな　□shriek 悲鳴を上げる　□brutal 残忍な　□cruelty 残酷さ　□desert 〜を見捨てる　□humane 人間味のある

delight his concern about water and sunshine, his feuds with parasites, his horror of frosts, his anxiety when the buds come slowly, his rapture when the leaves attain their lustre. In the East the art of floriculture is a very ancient one, and the loves of a poet and his favourite plant have often been recorded in story and song. With the development of ceramics during the Tang and Sung dynasties we hear of wonderful receptacles made to hold plants, not pots, but jewelled palaces. A special attendant was detailed to wait upon each flower and to wash its leaves with soft brushes made of rabbit hair. It has been written that the peony should be bathed by a handsome maiden in full costume, that a winter-plum should be watered by a pale, slender monk. In Japan, one of the most popular of the No-dances, the Hachinoki, composed during the Ashikaga period, is based upon the story of an

---

□ feud 抗争　□ parasite 寄生生物　□ frost 霜　□ rapture 歓喜　□ lustre つや　□ floriculture 草花栽培　□ receptacle 容器　□ peony 牡丹《植物》　□ winter-plum 寒梅《寒中に咲く梅》　□ No-dance 能の舞い　□ Hachinoki『鉢の木』《観阿弥の作と伝わる演目》　□ Ashikaga period 足利時代《1336-1573》

impoverished knight, who, on a freezing night, in lack of fuel for a fire, cuts his cherished plants in order to entertain a wandering friar. The friar is in reality no other than Hojo-Toki-yori, the Haroun-Al-Raschid of our tales, and the sacrifice is not without its reward. This opera never fails to draw tears from a Tokio audience even today.

Great precautions were taken for the preservation of delicate blossoms. Emperor Huensung, of the Tang dynasty, hung tiny golden bells on the branches in his garden to keep off the birds. He it was who went off in the springtime with his court musicians to gladden the flowers with soft music. A quaint tablet, which tradition ascribes to Yoshitsune, the hero of our Arthurian legends, is still extant in one of the Japanese monasteries. It is a notice put up for the protection of a certain wonderful plum-tree,

---

□ impoverished 貧しい　□ friar 托鉢僧　□ Hojo-Toki-yori 北条時頼《1227–1263、鎌倉幕府第五代執権》　□ Haroun-Al-Raschid ハールーン・アッラシード《766–809、アッバース朝の帝王》　□ Tokio 東京　□ precaution 予防措置　□ preservation 保護　□ Emperor Huensung 玄宗帝《685–762、中国唐時代の皇帝》　□ gladden ～を喜ばせる　□ ascribe to ～のものと見なす　□ Yoshitsune 源義経《1159–1189、平安時代末期の武将》　□ Arthurian legend アーサー王伝説　□ extant 現存している　□ plum-tree 梅の木

and appeals to us with the grim humour of a warlike age. After referring to the beauty of the blossoms, the inscription says: "Whoever cuts a single branch of this tree shall forfeit a finger therefor." Would that such laws could be enforced nowadays against those who wantonly destroy flowers and mutilate objects of art!

Yet even in the case of pot flowers we are inclined to suspect the selfishness of man. Why take the plants from their homes and ask them to bloom mid strange surroundings? Is it not like asking the birds to sing and mate cooped up in cages? Who knows but that the orchids feel stifled by the artificial heat in your conservatories and hopelessly long for a glimpse of their own Southern skies?

The ideal lover of flowers is he who visits them in their native haunts, like Taoyuen-ming, who sat before a broken bamboo fence in

□ grim 残酷な　□ warlike 戦乱の世の　□ inscription 記された文　□ forfeit ～を失う　□ therefor そのために　□ wantonly みだりに　□ mutilate ～を損傷させる　□ coope up 閉じ込める　□ orchids ラン《植物》　□ conservatory 温室　□ haunt 生息地　□ Taoyuen-ming 陶淵明《365–427、中国六朝時代の詩人》

converse with the wild chrysanthemum, or Linwosing, losing himself amid mysterious fragrance as he wandered in the twilight among the plum-blossoms of the Western Lake. 'Tis said that Chowmushih slept in a boat so that his dreams might mingle with those of the lotus. It was this same spirit which moved the Empress Komio, one of our most renowned Nara sovereigns, as she sang: "If I pluck thee, my hand will defile thee, O Flower! Standing in the meadows as thou art, I offer thee to the Buddhas of the past, of the present, of the future."

However, let us not be too sentimental. Let us be less luxurious but more magnificent. Said Laotse: "Heaven and earth are pitiless." Said Kobodaishi: "Flow, flow, flow, flow, the current of life is ever onward. Die, die, die, die, death comes to all." Destruction faces us wherever we turn. Destruction below and above, destruction

---

☐ Linwosing 林和靖《967-1028、中国宋時代の詩人》 ☐ Chowmushih 周茂叔《1017-1073、宋代の儒学者》 ☐ Empress Komio 光明皇后《701-760、聖武天皇の皇后》 ☐ renowned 名高い ☐ Nara sovereign 奈良時代の統治者 ☐ thee 汝《YOUの古語、目的格》 ☐ defile ～を汚す ☐ meadow 草地 ☐ sentimental 感傷的な ☐ luxurious ぜいたくな ☐ magnificent 壮大な ☐ pitiless 無慈悲な ☐ Kobodaishi 弘法大師《774-835、真言宗の開祖空海》 ☐ onward 前へ進んで

behind and before. Change is the only Eternal,—why not as welcome Death as Life? They are but counterparts one of the other,—the Night and Day of Brahma. Through the disintegration of the old, re-creation becomes possible. We have worshipped Death, the relentless goddess of mercy, under many different names. It was the shadow of the All-devouring that the Gheburs greeted in the fire. It is the icy purism of the sword-soul before which Shinto-Japan prostrates herself even today. The mystic fire consumes our weakness, the sacred sword cleaves the bondage of desire. From our ashes springs the phoenix of celestial hope, out of the freedom comes a higher realisation of manhood.

Why not destroy flowers if thereby we can evolve new forms ennobling the world idea? We only ask them to join in our sacrifice to the beautiful. We shall atone for the deed by consecrating ourselves to Purity and Simplicity. Thus reasoned the tea-masters when they established the Cult of Flowers.

Anyone acquainted with the ways of our tea and flower-masters must have noticed the religious veneration with which they regard flowers. They do not cull at random, but carefully select each branch or spray with an eye to the artistic composition they have in mind. They would be ashamed should they chance to cut more than were absolutely necessary. It may be remarked in this connection that they always associate the leaves, if there be any, with the flower, for their object is to present the whole beauty of plant life. In this respect, as in many others, their method differs from that pursued in Western countries. Here we are apt to see only the flower stems, heads, as it were, without body, stuck promiscuously into a vase.

□ acquainted with 〜に精通している　□ cull（花などを）つむ
□ promiscuously 乱雑に

When a tea-master has arranged a flower to his satisfaction he will place it on the tokonoma, the place of honour in a Japanese room. Nothing else will be placed near it which might interfere with its effect, not even a painting, unless there be some special æsthetic reason for the combination. It rests there like an enthroned prince, and the guests or disciples on entering the room will salute it with a profound bow before making their addresses to the host. Drawings from master-pieces are made and published for the edification of amateurs. The amount of literature on the subject is quite voluminous. When the flower fades, the master tenderly consigns it to the river or carefully buries it in the ground. Monuments even are sometimes erected to their memory.

The birth of the Art of Flower Arrangement seems to be simultaneous with that of Teaism

□ interfere 邪魔をする　□ enthroned 王位に就く　□ bow おじぎ
□ voluminous 著作の多い　□ tenderly そっと　□ consign 委ねる
□ monument 記念碑　□ Art of Flower Arrangement 華道　□ simultaneous 同時に起こる

in the fifteenth century. Our legends ascribe the first flower arrangement to those early Buddhist saints who gathered the flowers strewn by the storm and, in their infinite solicitude for all living things, placed them in vessels of water. It is said that Soami, the great painter and connoisseur of the court of Ashikaga-Yoshimasa, was one of the earliest adepts at it. Juko, the tea-master, was one of his pupils, as was also Senno, the founder of the house of Ikenobo, a family as illustrious in the annals of flowers as was that of the Kanos in painting. With the perfecting of the tea-ritual under Rikiu, in the latter part of the sixteenth century, flower arrangement also attains its full growth. Rikiu and his successors, the celebrated Oda-Wuraku, Furuta-Oribe, Koyetsu, Kobori-Enshiu, Katagiri-Sekishiu, vied with each other in forming new combinations. We must remember, however, that

---

☐ strewn STREY（まき散らす）の過去分詞　☐ solicitude 心遣い　☐ Soami 相阿弥《?–1525、室町時代後期の画家》　☐ connoisseur 鑑定家　☐ adept 名人　☐ Juko 珠光《1423–1502、侘茶の祖》　☐ Senno 専能《池坊の開祖》　☐ Ikenobo 池坊《華道家元、日本最古かつ最大の流派》　☐ Kanos 狩野派《15世紀–19世紀、日本絵画最大の画派》　☐ Oda-Wuraku 織田有楽《1547–1622、大名》　☐ Furuta-Oribe 古田織部《1543–1615、大名》　☐ Koyetsu 光悦《1558–1637、書家、陶芸家、芸術家》　☐ Katagiri-Sekishiu 片桐石州《1605–1673、大名》

the flower worship of the tea-masters formed only a part of their æsthetic ritual, and was not a distinct religion by itself. A flower arrangement, like the other works of art in the tea-room, was subordinated to the total scheme of decoration. Thus Sekishiu ordained that white plum blossoms should not be made use of when snow lay in the garden. "Noisy" flowers were relentlessly banished from the tea-room. A flower arrangement by a teamaster loses its significance if removed from the place for which it was originally intended, for its lines and proportions have been specially worked out with a view to its surroundings.

The adoration of the flower for its own sake begins with the rise of "Flower-Masters," toward the middle of the seventeenth century. It now becomes independent of the tea-room and knows no law save that the vase imposes

---

☐ subordinate 〜を従属させる ☐ relentlessly 容赦なく ☐ banish 追い出す
☐ Flower-Master 花の宗匠 ☐ impose 強要する

on it. New conceptions and methods of execution now become possible, and many were the principles and schools resulting therefrom. A writer in the middle of the last century said he could count over one hundred different schools of flower arrangement. Broadly speaking, these divide themselves into two main branches, the Formalistic and the Naturalesque. The Formalistic schools, led by the Ikenobos, aimed at a classic idealism corresponding to that of the Kano-academicians. We possess records of arrangements by the early masters of this school which almost reproduce the flower paintings of Sansetsu and Tsunenobu. The Naturalesque school, on the other hand, as its name implies, accepted nature as its model, only imposing such modifications of form as conduced to the expression of artistic unity. Thus we recognise in its works the same

□ execution 創作　□ therefrom そこから《古》　□ Formalistic 形式派
□ Naturalesque 写実派　□ correspond 〜に相当する　□ Sansetsu 山雪《1590-1651、狩野派の画家》　□ Tsunenobu 常信《1636-1713、狩野派の画家》
□ modification 改良すること　□ conduce to 〜をもたらす　□ Shijo school 四条派《呉春を祖とする日本画の一派》

impulses which formed the Ukiyoe and Shijo schools of painting.

It would be interesting, had we time, to enter more fully than is now possible into the laws of composition and detail formulated by the various flower-masters of this period, showing, as they would, the fundamental theories which governed Tokugawa decoration. We find them referring to the Leading Principle (Heaven), the Subordinate Principle (Earth), the Reconciling Principle (Man), and any flower arrangement which did not embody these principles was considered barren and dead. They also dwelt much on the importance of treating a flower in its three different aspects, the Formal, the Semi-Formal, and the Informal. The first might be said to represent flowers in the stately costume of the ballroom, the second in the easy elegance of afternoon

---

□ formulate 〜を定式化する　□ Leading Principle (Heaven) 指導する原理（天）　□ Subordinate Principle (Earth) 従属する原理（地）　□ Reconciling Principle (Man) 和解する原理（人）　□ formal 正式　□ semi-formal 半正式　□ informal 略式　□ stately 風格ある　□ dishabille 略装

dress, the third in the charming dishabille of the boudoir.

Our personal sympathies are with the flower-arrangements of the tea-master rather than with those of the flower-master. The former is art in its proper setting and appeals to us on account of its true intimacy with life. We should like to call this school the Natural in contradistinction to the Naturalesque and Formalistic schools. The teamaster deems his duty ended with the selection of the flowers, and leaves them to tell their own story. Entering a tea-room in late winter, you may see a slender spray of wild cherries in combination with a budding camellia; it is an echo of departing winter coupled with the prophecy of spring. Again, if you go into a noon-tea on some irritatingly hot summer day, you may discover in the darkened coolness of the tokonoma a single lily in a hanging vase;

☐ intimacy 親密さ　☐ budding 蕾の　☐ prophecy お告げ　☐ irritatingly 苛立つほどに

dripping with dew, it seems to smile at the foolishness of life.

A solo of flowers is interesting, but in a concerto with painting and sculpture the combination becomes entrancing. Sekishiu once placed some water plants in a flat receptacle to suggest the vegetation of lakes and marshes, and on the wall above he hung a painting by Soami of wild ducks flying in the air. Shoha, another tea-master, combined a poem on the Beauty of Solitude by the Sea with a bronze incense burner in the form of a fisherman's hut and some wild flowers of the beach. One of the guests has recorded that he felt in the whole composition the breath of waning autumn.

Flower stories are endless. We shall re-count but one more. In the sixteenth century the morning-glory was as yet a rare plant with us. Rikiu had an entire garden planted with it,

☐ concerto 協奏曲 ☐ entrancing うっとりさせる ☐ vegetation 草木
☐ marsh 沼池 ☐ Shoha 紹巴《1525-1602、戦国時代の歌人》 ☐ Beauty of Solitude by the Sea 海辺のわびしい美しさ ☐ morning-glory アサガオ
☐ assiduous 根気強い ☐ convolvuli ヒルガオ

which he cultivated with assiduous care. The fame of his convolvuli reached the ear of the Taiko, and he expressed a desire to see them, in consequence of which Rikiu invited him to a morning tea at his house. On the appointed day the Taiko walked through the garden, but nowhere could he see any vestige of the convolvulus. The ground had been leveled and strewn with fine pebbles and sand. With sullen anger the despot entered the tearoom, but a sight waited him there which completely restored his humour. On the tokonoma, in a rare bronze of Sung workmanship, lay a single morning-glory—the queen of the whole garden!

In such instances we see the full significance of the Flower Sacrifice. Perhaps the flowers appreciated the full significance of it. They are not cowards, like men. Some flowers glory in death—certainly the Japanese cherry blossoms

☐ sullen 不機嫌な   ☐ despot 独裁者

do, as they freely surrender themselves to the winds. Anyone who has stood before the fragrant avalanche at Yoshino or Arashiyama must have realised this. For a moment they hover like bejewelled clouds and dance above the crystal streams; then, as they sail away on the laughing waters, they seem to say: "Farewell, O Spring! We are on to Eternity."

☐ hover 浮かぶ ☐ bejewelled 宝石を散りばめた

Chapter 7
Tea-Masters

Tea-Masters

Real appreciation of art only possible to those who make of it a living influence – Contributions of the Tea-Masters to art – Their influence on the conduct of life – The Last Tea of Rikiu

*I*n religion the Future is behind us. In art the Present is the eternal. The tea-master held that real appreciation of art is only possible to those who make of it a living influence. Thus they sought to regulate their daily life by the high standard of refinement which obtained in the tea-room. In all circumstances serenity of mind should be maintained, and conversation should be so conducted as never to mar the harmony of the surroundings. The cut and colour of the dress, the poise of the body, and the manner of walking could all be made expressions of artistic personality. These were matters not to be lightly ignored, for until one has made himself beautiful he has no right to approach beauty. Thus the tea-master strove to be something more than the artist,—art itself. It was the Zen of æstheticism. Perfection is everywhere if we only choose to recognise it. Rikiu loved to quote

□ regulate 〜を律する □ circumstance 状況 □ poise 平衡状態 □ strove STRIVE（努力する）の過去 □ quote 引用する

an old poem which says: "To those who long only for flowers, fain would I show the full-blown spring which abides in the toiling buds of snow-covered hills"

Manifold indeed have been the contributions of the tea-masters to art. They completely revolutionised the classical architecture and interior decorations, and established the new style which we have described in the chapter of the tea-room, a style to whose influence even the palaces and monasteries built after the sixteenth century have all been subject. The many-sided Kobori-Enshiu has left notable examples of his genius in the Imperial villa of Katsura, the castles of Nagoya and Nijo, and the monastery of Kohoan. All the celebrated gardens of Japan were laid out by the tea-masters. Our pottery would probably never have attained its high quality of excellence if the tea-masters had not

☐ abide in 〜に住む ☐ toil 骨折って働く ☐ manifold 多様性
☐ revolutionise 〜を大改革する ☐ Imperial villa of Katsura 桂離宮《京都にある皇族関連施設》 ☐ monastery of Kohoan 孤篷庵《京都にある寺院》
☐ pottery 陶器 ☐ attain 到達する

lent to it their inspiration, the manufacture of the utensils used in the tea-ceremony calling forth the utmost expenditure of ingenuity on the part of our ceramists. The Seven Kilns of Enshiu are well known to all students of Japanese pottery. Many of our textile fabrics bear the names of tea-masters who conceived their colour or design. It is impossible, indeed, to find any department of art in which the tea-masters have not left marks of their genius. In painting and lacquer it seems almost superfluous to mention the immense service they have rendered. One of the greatest schools of painting owes its origin to the tea-master Honnami-Koyetsu, famed also as a lacquer artist and potter. Beside his works, the splendid creation of his grandson, Koho, and of his grand-nephews, Korin and Ken-zan, almost fall into the shade. The whole Korin school, as it is generally designated, is an expression

---

□ utensil 道具　□ The Seven Kilns of Enshiu 遠州七窯《茶器の名産地である7箇所》　□ superfluous 過分な　□ Honnami-Koyetsu 本阿弥光悦《1558-1637、書家、陶芸家、芸術家》　□ Koho 好甫《1601-1682、芸術家》　□ Korin 光琳《1658-1716、画家、工芸家》　□ Ken-zan 乾山《1663-1743、陶工、画家》

of Teaism. In the broad lines of this school we seem to find the vitality of nature herself.

Great as has been the influence of the tea-masters in the field of art, it is as nothing compared to that which they have exerted on the conduct of life. Not only in the usages of polite society, but also in the arrangement of all our domestic details, do we feel the presence of the tea-masters. Many of our delicate dishes, as well as our way of serving food, are their inventions. They have taught us to dress only in garments of sober colours. They have instructed us in the proper spirit in which to approach flowers. They have given emphasis to our natural love of simplicity, and shown us the beauty of humility. In fact, through their teachings tea has entered the life of the people.

Those of us who know not the secret of properly regulating our own existence on this

□ exert 影響を与える □ garment 衣服

tumultuous sea of foolish troubles which we call life are constantly in a state of misery while vainly trying to appear happy and contented. We stagger in the attempt to keep our moral equilibrium, and see forerunners of the tempest in every cloud that floats on the horizon. Yet there is joy and beauty in the roll of the billows as they sweep outward toward eternity. Why not enter into their spirit, or, like Liehtse, ride upon the hurricane itself?

He only who has lived with the beautiful can die beautifully. The last moments of the great tea-masters were as full of exquisite refinement as had been their lives. Seeking always to be in harmony with the great rhythm of the universe, they were ever prepared to enter the unknown. The "Last Tea of Rikiu" will stand forth forever as the acme of tragic grandeur.

Long had been the friendship between Rikiu and the Taiko-Hideyoshi, and high the

---

□ tumultuous 嵐のような □ stagger ぐらつく □ equilibrium 落ち着き
□ tempest 大嵐 □ "Last Tea of Rikiu" 利休の最後の一服

estimation in which the great warrior held the tea-master. But the friendship of a despot is ever a dangerous honour. It was an age rife with treachery, and men trusted not even their nearest kin. Rikiu was no servile courtier, and had often dared to differ in argument with his fierce patron. Taking advantage of the coldness which had for some time existed between the Taiko and Rikiu, the enemies of the latter accused him of being implicated in a conspiracy to poison the despot. It was whispered to Hideyoshi that the fatal potion was to be administered to him with a cup of the green beverage prepared by the tea-master. With Hideyoshi suspicion was sufficient ground for instant execution, and there was no appeal from the will of the angry ruler. One privilege alone was granted to the condemned—the honour of dying by his own hand.

On the day destined for his self-immolation,

☐ estimation 高い評価　☐ rife はびこって　☐ treachery 裏切り行為　☐ servile 媚びへつらう　☐ courtier ご機嫌取り　☐ implicate 〜に関与させる　☐ conspiracy 陰謀　☐ sufficient ground 十分な根拠　☐ destined 運命づけられた　☐ self-immolation 自害

Rikiu invited his chief disciples to a last tea-ceremony. Mournfully at the appointed time the guests met at the portico. As they look into the garden path the trees seem to shudder, and in the rustling of their leaves are heard the whispers of homeless ghosts. Like solemn sentinels before the gates of Hades stand the grey stone lanterns. A wave of rare incense is wafted from the tea-room; it is the summons which bids the guests to enter. One by one they advance and take their places. In the tokonoma hangs a kakemono,—a wonderful writing by an ancient monk dealing with the evanescence of all earthly things. The singing kettle, as it boils over the brazier, sounds like some cicada pouring forth his woes to departing summer. Soon the host enters the room. Each in turn is served with tea, and each in turn silently drains his cup, the host last of all. According to established etiquette, the

□ mournfully 悲しげに　□ solemn いかめしい　□ sentinel 番人　□ Hades ハデス《ギリシア神話の冥界の王》　□ waft 〜を漂わせる　□ brazier 火鉢
□ cicada セミ

chief guest now asks permission to examine the tea-equipage. Rikiu places the various articles before them with the kakemono. After all have expressed admiration of their beauty, Rikiu presents one of them to each of the assembled company as a souvenir. The bowl alone he keeps.

"Never again shall this cup, polluted by the lips of misfortune, be used by man." He speaks, and breaks the vessel into fragments.

The ceremony is over; the guests with difficulty restraining their tears, take their last farewell and leave the room. One only, the nearest and dearest, is requested to remain and witness the end. Rikiu then removes his tea-gown and carefully folds it upon the mat, thereby disclosing the immaculate white death robe which it had hitherto concealed. Tenderly he gazes on the shining blade of the fatal dagger, and in exquisite verse thus addresses it:

☐ pollute 〜を汚染する ☐ misfortune 不運 ☐ fragment 破片 ☐ restrain 〜を抑える ☐ dagger 短刀

Welcome to thee,
O sword of eternity!
Through Buddha
And through Dharuma alike
Thou hast cleft thy way.

With a smile upon his face Rikiu passed forth into the unknown.

☐ hast HAVE の古語 ☐ cleft CLEAVE (突き進む) の過去・過去分詞 ☐ thy そなたの《古》 ☐ pass 亡くなる

Tea Ceremony
茶の湯

Tea Utensils 茶道具

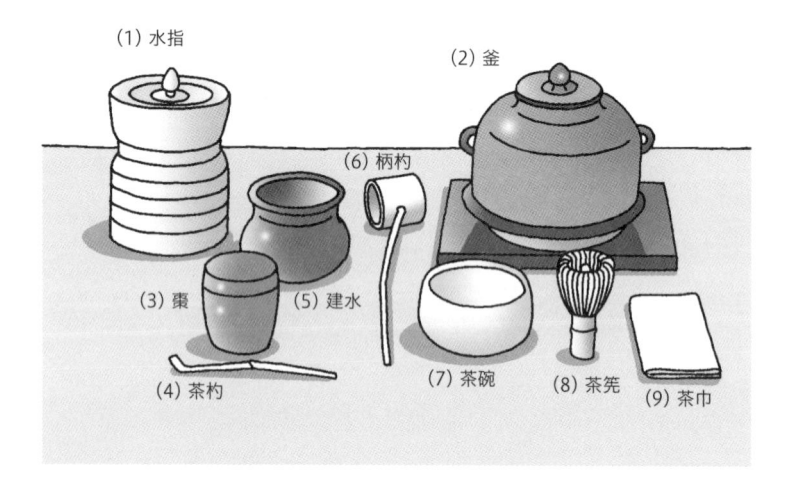

(1) 水指
(2) 釜
(3) 棗
(4) 茶杓
(5) 建水
(6) 柄杓
(7) 茶碗
(8) 茶筅
(9) 茶巾

1, *mizusashi,* Jug of water

2, *kama,* Kettle and brazier

3, *natsume,* Lacquerware container for powdered green tea

4, *chashaku,* Tea scoop, used to transfer powdered tea from the natsume to the teabowl

5, *kensui,* Basin for used water

6, *hishaku,* Water ladle

7, *chawan,* Teabowl

8, *chasen,* Split bamboo tea whisk, used to whip the powdered tea with water

9, *chakin,* Tea cloth

Tearoom 茶室

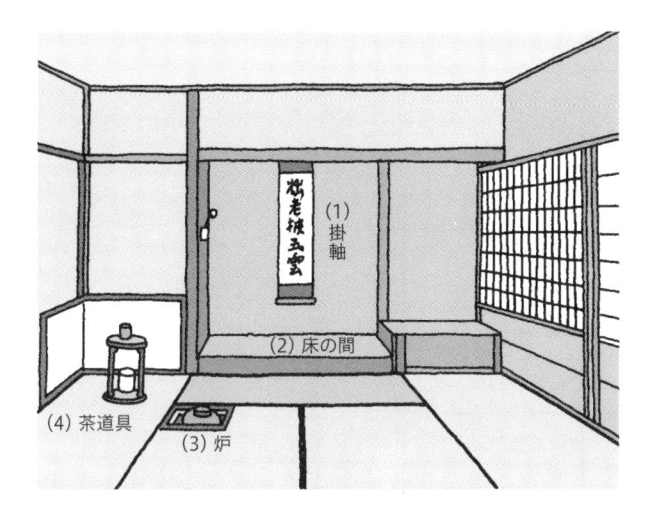

1, *kakejiku,* Scroll
2, 5, *tokonoma,* Alcove
3, 6, *ro,* Hearth
4, *chadogu,* Tea utensils
7, *mizuya,* Room for tea and food preparation
8, *tsuginoma,* Afterroom
9, *iriguchi,* Main entrance, used by the guests
10, *kamiza,* Top seat
11, *shimoza,* Lower seat

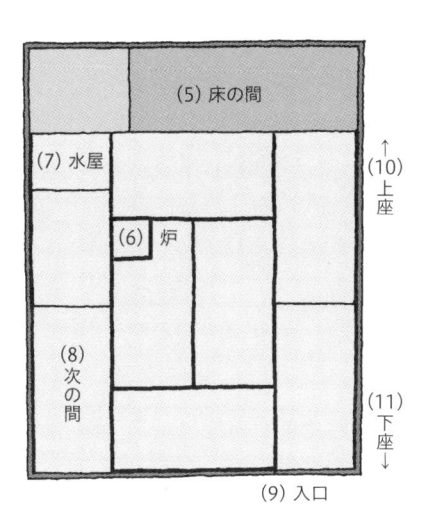

Tea Ceremony

Taking Your Seat　席入りの手順

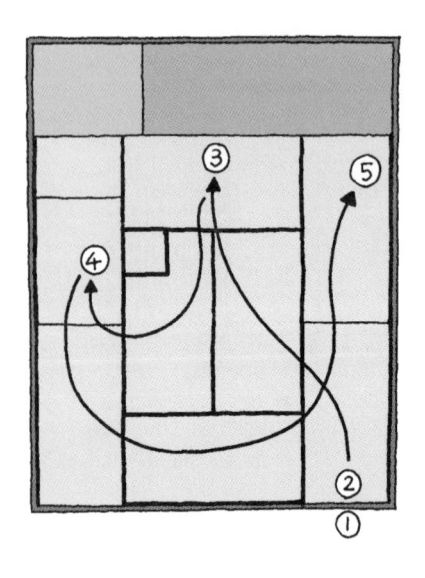

① 入り口の襖を開け、扇子を前に置いて、かるく会釈
Open the *fusuma* at the entrance, place your fan (*sensu*) in front, and bow slightly.

② にじって敷居を越す
Edge forward over the threshold.

③　床正面に座り、かるく手をついて掛物を拝見
Sitting in front of the alcove, place your hands lightly on the *tatami*, and admire the hanging scroll.

④　道具畳に座り、釜、炉縁を拝見
Sitting in the afterroom, admire the kettle and brazier.

⑤　正客の座に進み、足を揃えて座る
Proceed to the position for the first guest and sit with legs arranged properly.

⑥　亭主を迎え、挨拶をする
Greet the host with a bow.

Making the Tea お茶を点てる

① 入り口に座り、一礼
Sitting in the entrance, bow as a sign of respect.

② 炉の前に座り、茶道具を揃える
Sit in front of the hearth and arrange the utensils.

③ 茶碗、茶筅を前に置く
Place the teabowl and whisk in front of you.

④ いちど茶碗にお湯を入れ、建水に捨ててから、茶碗を拭く
Pour hot water into the teabowl, empty the water into the basin for that purpose, and wipe the teabowl.

⑤ お茶を2杓すくい、茶碗に入れる
Scoop two spoonfuls of powered tea into the teabowl.

⑥ 柄杓でお湯を茶碗に入れる
Ladle hot water into the teabowl (3.5 ladlefuls).

⑦ お茶を点てる
Whisk the teabowl into a fine froth.

⑧ 茶碗の正面を客に向けて出す
Facing forward, offer the teabowl to the guest.

Drinking the Tea お茶の飲み方

① お茶が出されると、茶碗をとって、膝前に仮置きする
Pick up the teabowl and place it in front of your knees.

② 正客の座に戻り、茶碗を次客との間において。「お先に」と次礼する
Return to your position and place the bowl between yourself and the second guest, saying, "Pardon me [for drinking before you]."

③ 茶碗をとり、感謝の気持ちを込めておしいだく
Taking up the bowl, drink for the first time with a feeling of gratitude.

④ 茶碗を手前に2度回して、正面を左横に向けて、3口半ほどで飲みきりする
Rotate the bowl once, and with the front of the bowl facing to the left, first take a sip and then finish the rest.

⑤ 飲み口を親指と人差し指で左から右へ拭く
With your thumb and index finger, wipe from left to right the place where your lips touched the bowl.

⑥ 茶碗を拝見する
Admire the bowl.

⑦ 茶碗の正面を向こうに回してから返す
Rotate the teabowl so that the front is facing away from you and return it to the host.

The Book of Tea
英文版 茶の本

2015年4月4日　第1刷発行

著　者　　岡倉 天心
発行者　　浦 晋亮
発行所　　IBC パブリッシング株式会社
　　　　　〒162-0804 東京都新宿区中里町29番3号　菱秀神楽坂ビル9F
　　　　　Tel. 03-3513-4511　Fax. 03-3513-4512
　　　　　www.ibcpub.co.jp

印刷所　　株式会社シナノパブリッシングプレス

© IBC Publishing, Inc. 2015
Printed in Japan

落丁本・乱丁本は、小社宛にお送りください。送料小社負担にてお取り替えいたします。
本書の無断複写（コピー）は著作権法上での例外を除き禁じられています。

ISBN978-4-7946-0338-8